The Forensic Certified Public Accountant and the Halloween Identity Theft Ghost Employee -

Book Number Two

By Dwight David Thrash CPA FCPA CGMA

AUTHOR'S NOTE

The characters are fictional, even though they appear to be real. This book is based on real accounting and forensic accounting. The author is a real Certified Public Accountant, Forensic Certified Public Accountant, and a Chartered Global Management Accountant in good standing.

For my parents, Dwight A. and Wanda, & my sister, Delesa and her family,

Thank you, for your support.

I love you.

Contents

Chapter 1 Recap of Titus Uno, CPA FCPA CGMA, his Team, and Their Team Gadgets 6

Chapter 2 the Halloween Planner Company 17

Chapter 3 the Halloween Planner Company Headquarters 22

Chapter 4 the Halloween Planner Company Halloween Inventory Storage Building 26

Chapter 5 "Trick-or-Treat" Accounting for These Accounts 31

Chapter 6 Halloween Candies Accounting for These Accounts 36

Chapter 7 Halloween Costumes Accounting for These Accounts 41

Chapter 8 Haunted Houses or Haunted Mansions Accounting for These Accounts 45

Chapter 9 Halloween Decorations Accounting for These Accounts 50

Chapter 10 Halloween Parties Accounting for These Accounts 55

Chapter 11 Halloween Dances Accounting for These Accounts 59

Chapter 12 Halloween Movies Accounting for These Accounts 63

Chapter 13 Halloween Cards Accounting for These Accounts 67

Chapter 14 Halloween Mazes for These Accounts 71

Chapter 15 the Jack-O-Lanterns and Pumpkin Patches Accounting for These Accounts 76

Chapter 16 Surprise 80

Chapter 17 the Case of the Halloween "Identity Theft Ghost Employee" 85

Chapter 18 the Conclusion by Titus Uno CPA FCPA CGMA 88

Chapter 1 Recap of Titus Uno, CPA FCPA CGMA, his Team, and Their Team Gadgets

If you have not read *The Forensic Certified Public Accountant and the Cremated 64-SQUARES Financial Statements* Book Number One, I recommend that you do read it before this book because this is the second book in the series of *The Forensic Certified Public Accountant*...

... As described in *The Forensic Certified Public Accountant and the Cremated 64-SQUARES Financial Statements* - book number one: Let me tell you a little bit about myself starting with my education. I, Titus Uno, Certified Public Accountant, Forensic Certified Public Accountant, and Chartered Global Management Accountant, have many years of accounting education and experience that has prepared me for terrible international crime.

As described in *The Forensic Certified Public Accountant and the Cremated 64-SQUARES Financial Statements* - book number one: Now I, Titus Uno, Certified Public Accountant, Forensic Certified Public Accountant, and Chartered Global Management Accountant, will share information about my family life. I am still single, but on the lookout for a nice Christian wife. Having a nice Christian family and friends are what makes life great. I, Titus Uno, Certified Public Accountant, Forensic Certified Public Accountant, and Chartered Global Management Accountant, am active in my church by playing first trumpet in the church orchestra and teaching the young career singles department. I also play the trumpet in the local community band. I really enjoy playing the trumpet. I, Titus Uno, Certified Public Accountant, Forensic Certified Public Accountant, and Chartered Global Management Accountant, also plays the piano just for fun. At church everyone helps each other so that everyone can be the best person that they can be by helping others that need help. This is a great cycle to be in which is being nice and helping each other by being nice thus nice produces nice. So be nice every chance you get.

As described in *The Forensic Certified Public Accountant and the Cremated 64-SQUARES Financial Statements* - book number one: First, Drew Samson is a Private Investigator that enjoys going undercover to gather information (both tangible and intangible are useful) for me to help me solve the case that we are working on to help me decide who is guilty. Drew Samson has many years of experience at being a detective to get to the truth. Drew Samson spent several years working in a police department, working his way up to detective in the police department. Drew Samson spent hours and hours tracking down leads on several police cases at the same time. Drew Samson finally decided to find a job that would allow him to focus on one huge case. These huge case would put criminals that committed worse crimes behind bars for several years. When Drew Samson heard that I, Titus Uno, Certified Public Accountant, Forensic Certified Public Accountant, and Chartered Global Management Accountant, was looking for a P.I. or in private investigator, Drew Samson sent me his impressive resume that contained his vast knowledge and experience as a detective of the police department. That is what I was looking for in the private investigator of my Forensic Certified Public Accountant team. So I decided to hire Drew Samson as the P.I of my team.

As described in *The Forensic Certified Public Accountant and the Cremated 64-SQUARES Financial Statements* - book number one: Drew Samson has a beautiful wife, Jill Samson, and 2 children, Simon Samson, a boy, who is ten and Delilah Samson, a girl, who is 8. Drew Samson works hard to support his family, while having the flexibility to see his children in the activities. It is great that Drew Samson has this job and a family.

As described in *The Forensic Certified Public Accountant and the Cremated 64-SQUARES Financial Statements* - book number one: Second, Dena Hope, is the computer programmer and genius. Dena Hope has a Doctorate Degree in computer science and like Drew Samson is very experienced. Her resume is full of Fortune 500 companies and government agencies that Dena Hope has helped build firewalls to prevent hackers. She also studies the worst computer viruses, and helps companies stop and fix the computer worms. She is a respected computer programmer.

As described in *The Forensic Certified Public Accountant and the Cremated 64-SQUARES Financial Statements* - book number one: Dena Hope is single because she spent her time working really hard. That is why Dena Hope is one of the best computer programmers in the world. Dena Hope dedicates all of her free time working on the computer. Dena Hope designs computer programs just fort the fun of designing programs that work. Some of the computer programs that Dena Hope writes are very simple programs, but other computer programs are very difficult programs. Simple programs include coin flipping or two choice programs. While complex programs include using macros to write the most difficult computer programs such as those used in computer games with 3D graphics that are so clear and realistic that it looks real.

As described in *The Forensic Certified Public Accountant and the Cremated 64-SQUARES Financial Statements* - book number one: Third, Veronica Jackson, the scheduler, organizer, and item collector for the team. Without her the operations of my team would not be possible. Every team need an organizer and a go getter. Veronica Jackson sets up the meeting and makes sure that we get to that meet on time. Veronica Jackson always helps us appear to be great by keeping up punctual and organized. There is nothing more embarrassing that being late to meet to interview a suspected quilt criminal and expect them to divulge pertinent incriminating information about the crime or perhaps lead us on another lead about something someone has done that would take the heat off of them.

As described in *The Forensic Certified Public Accountant and the Cremated 64-SQUARES Financial Statements* - book number one: Veronica Jackson, believe it or not, worked for the President of the United States as one of his secretaries. I, Titus Uno, Certified Public Accountant, Forensic Certified Public Accountant, and Chartered Global Management Accountant, would say that this makes her references one of the best. It was hard to believe, but it turned out to be true. That is why when I, Titus Uno, Certified Public Accountant, Forensic Certified Public Accountant, and Chartered Global Management Accountant, say that, "Veronica Jackson can get thing accomplished." It is really true. There was this one time that we needed to get an invitation to an invitation only event in Washington, D.C. Veronica Jackson pull it off and got the Forensic Certified Public Accountant team the invitation. It is nice to have friends in high places. I, Titus Uno, Certified Public Accountant, Forensic Certified Public Accountant, and Chartered Global Management Accountant, would like to just say that Veronica Jackson's list of contacts is very long.

As described in *The Forensic Certified Public Accountant and the Cremated 64-SQUARES Financial Statements* - book number one: Veronica Jackson is happily married to her husband, Carl Jackson for 24 years. They have a daughter, Rose Jackson that has just graduated from college with a Master's Degree in Accounting. Carl and Veronica Jackson are very proud of Rose Jackson. She already has a job at one of the Big 4 accounting firms in the United States of America. Becoming a successful Certified Public Accountant has always been the goal of Rose Jackson. Veronica Jackson has been training for the Certified Public Accountant Examination for years and especially while she was in college getting an education.

As described in *The Forensic Certified Public Accountant and the Cremated 64-SQUARES Financial Statements* - book number one: My team uses the most high technology available such as: cameras to take pictures, drones to take videos, cell phones to communicate, Global Positioning System chips to track where suspects travel, night vision binoculars that deer hunters use and supersonic listening devices like those used at football games, ear piece combined with shades recorders to communicate with each other, polygraph machines to get to the truth, and wiretaps to gather information about the company, its employees to make it possible to reconstruct the financials and to help assist in the prosecution of the crime. This high technology is exciting to use because spying on people is fun. The information that is discovered has to be pieced together so that it makes sense. Each gadget mentioned above will have statements about the gadget, then an example of when my team used that piece of equipment was used in previous cases.

As described in *The Forensic Certified Public Accountant and the Cremated 64-SQUARES Financial Statements* - book number one: Cameras to take pictures and videos. "A picture is worth a thousand words." That statement is so true. Videos are picture after picture. It can be used to prove that someone is lying and turn a case in another direction. There are video and photo cameras everywhere and a great detective can locate photo with great ease. There are even cameras that take pictures of drivers as they run red lights.

As described in *The Forensic Certified Public Accountant and the Cremated 64-SQUARES Financial Statements* - book number one: Cameras were used by my team to track down a person that my team needed to interrogate because they had knowledge about some inventory that had been stolen.

As described in *The Forensic Certified Public Accountant and the Cremated 64-SQUARES Financial Statements* - book number one: Drones to take videos. Wow, video cameras in the sky. This is such an exciting piece of spy technology because it has the capabilities to go to areas without being detected. The main thing that you have to worry about is that you do not fly the drone in restricted areas. You also have to be an experienced drone flyer because if you are not experienced then you may hit objects and crash. Drones are great spy gadgets, but you have to be able to operate it legally and safely.

As described in *The Forensic Certified Public Accountant and the Cremated 64-SQUARES Financial Statements* - book number one: Drones allowed my team to go to an area that they normally could not get into to gain an important piece of information. For example, there was this one time that a person was pretending that they had gotten hurt at work so that they could get workers' compensation. My team was hired to see if the employee was really hurt or if the employee was faking their injuries. The drone caught the employee mowing their backyard using a push mower. Case closed. I, Titus Uno, Certified Public Accountant, Forensic Certified Public Accountant, and Chartered Global Management Accountant, did not even have to show up to testify, the case was settled out of court. That employee is not working there anymore.

As described in *The Forensic Certified Public Accountant and the Cremated 64-SQUARES Financial Statements* - book number one: Cellphones to communicate, take photo as explained earlier. Cellphones can be cloned or bumped so that the owner may not ever be aware that their phone is being listened to by another person such as a detective.

As described in *The Forensic Certified Public Accountant and the Cremated 64-SQUARES Financial Statements* - book number one: Cellphones are used by my team all the time. My team used a cell phone to be able to listen to a conversation between the cellphone owner and the person that had been stealing from the company that hire me and my team for years. The stealer was being blackmailed by the cellphone owner. Let us just say this case was a two-for-one case.

As described in *The Forensic Certified Public Accountant and the Cremated 64-SQUARES Financial Statements* - book number one: Global Positioning System chips to track where suspects travel is very exciting. This is the Forensic Certified Public Accountant's best spy tool. They have gotten very tiny even microscopic. A great detective operates like a criminal pickpocket, except that detective places the microscopic chip on the suspect. Once the chip is on the suspect, the suspect is a moving duck and does not have a chance to escape the tracking device. The tracking device pinpoints the suspect down to the exact inch. This comes in handy because if the suspect is in a particular location, then that means that they cannot be in another location that the detective can search for items that may help solve the case.

As described in *The Forensic Certified Public Accountant and the Cremated 64-SQUARES Financial Statements* - book number one: My team uses Global Positioning System in almost every case. In a previous case, the Global Positioning System was placed on a helicopter of a suspected employee, who was suspected of using the helicopter for personal use instead of using the helicopter for just business, to see where the helicopter was flown during a period of a week. The helicopter was being used to fly tourists to location for a side business of the helicopter pilot. The company that the helicopter worked for was not happy and wanted me to testify to the court the amount that the company had lost since the two-timing helicopter pilot had been a pilot for the company.

As described in *The Forensic Certified Public Accountant and the Cremated 64-SQUARES Financial Statements* - book number one: Night vision binoculars that deer hunters use and bugs or supersonic listening devices like those used at football games when a judge has not authorized bugs to be planted. There are different ways to overhear information without the talking party being aware of the fact that they are being listened to by other people. The binoculars can be used to ascertain how many people are in building and where they are located. The supersonic listening devices are used to put words to the people in the building that are having the conversation.

As described in *The Forensic Certified Public Accountant and the Cremated 64-SQUARES Financial Statements* - book number one: My teams' use of night vision binoculars is very interesting. A college hired me and my team to help find a missing college mascot. A missing mascot is bad luck for the college and might cause the university to lose the game. Lost games equal lost revenue and lost revenue. Let me put it to you this way universities have to work for every penny in order to keep the university operating. So my team used the night vision binoculars to find the mascot in one of the Fraternity Houses of the opposing football teams. The university was not happy, and decided to press charges. I had to testify in court, what the best estimate of lost revenue that the lost mascot caused the university. This was a very unusual case, but a very interesting use of my team's and my time. This was "the missing mascot case."

As described in *The Forensic Certified Public Accountant and the Cremated 64-SQUARES Financial Statements* - book number one: Ear hearing piece that when connected with microphones make a great communicating devices between the person at the scene and their cover outside able to communicate verbally. Shades or pin recorders are also used to communicate visually with each other during a sting operation and to record the operation for pertinent information to the case. The ear piece has improved through the years. They can be concealed in the ear and if someone does see the ear hearing piece, they will just think that it is an ordinary hearing aid. "What did you say?" Microphones have gotten microscopic, also. We live in a world that whatever is said or done can be recorded. Shades are a very cool video camera that can be worn to record what is going on around the shade wearer and record at an external location. The people will not know that they are being recorded. They used to be regular black plastic with thick lenses to help hid the recording parts. There are also microscopic recording dots that can be placed on clothing. Like above, the people will not know that they are being recorded.

As described in *The Forensic Certified Public Accountant and the Cremated 64-SQUARES Financial Statements* - book number one: Ear hearing piece with microphones were very useful on a case that required that my team be on a stakeout, while a suspected embezzler was out of the house. Each team member had a set of ear hearing pieces and a microphone in order to communicate with each other. Communication is very important because the lives of the people that were are investigating have a high probability of being convinced and sentenced to Jail. While he was out of the house my team did a little search of the embezzler's house. Part of my team was outside as a lookout and used the microphone to communicate with the other team members that were inside gathering the important incriminating information that would send the embezzler to jail.

As described in *The Forensic Certified Public Accountant and the Cremated 64-SQUARES Financial Statements* - book number one: Polygraph machines to get to the truth. These machines can determine whether a suspect is actually telling the truth about facts that the questioner thinks that the suspect is lying about. There are ways to outsmart the polygraph machines, but it catches most suspects when they are lying.

As described in *The Forensic Certified Public Accountant and the Cremated 64-SQUARES Financial Statements* - book number one: Polygraph machines allowed my team to get a poker player that was beating the odds, after 30 minutes of my team using the polygraph machine just asking yes or no questions, to admit that that the poker player was in fact counting the cards. My team called this case "the case of the no poker face" because they got him to tell his tale or tell.

As described in *The Forensic Certified Public Accountant and the Cremated 64-SQUARES Financial Statements* - book number one: Wiretaps. Judges have to be convinced that there is probable cause to issue a wiretap on a suspected party's phone lines and computers. It is so much easier to tap cell phones and computers, than landline phones. Everyone's phones and computers are great sources of private information. For example, it is possible to hack a computer and see if someone has deposited an unexplained amount of money into their bank account, thereby raising a red flag that this person should be questioned about this fact. However, someone else might be questioned, so that the suspect will not be aware of the fact that they are a suspect. Thereby, allowing the suspect to stay in a relaxed state of mind, before being accused of the crime.

As described in *The Forensic Certified Public Accountant and the Cremated 64-SQUARES Financial Statements* - book number one: My team have used wiretaps on computers to find out important and useful information that might not otherwise be obtainable. My team used wiretaps on this one case to prove that an employee has top secret files that they had taken from their company in order to sell the files to their companies' competition. The employee set up a time to exchange the top secret files for $5,000,000.00 cash money in untraceable bills. My team got the time and place by using the wiretap that was on the Employee's computer. The employee was caught and sentenced to jail time thanks to my team and this high tech spy technology.

As described in *The Forensic Certified Public Accountant and the Cremated 64-SQUARES Financial Statements* - book number one: I, Titus Uno, Certified Public Accountant, Forensic

Certified Public Accountant, and Chartered Global Management Accountant, am privileged to tell you about a secret new gadget, so I hope that you will promise that you will not tell anybody else about this top secret gadget. Good, you will not tell anybody else about what I am going to divulge to you. It is contact lenses that can zoom in on a dime that is 100 yards away and you can read the writing on the face of the dime. It make spying that much more covert. The cost of each pair of contact lenses are $2,000.00. There is only one company that sells these covert contacts and right now only law officials, private investigators, and detectives or spies can purchase these covert contact lenses. These covert contact lenses are connected to a remote control device that enables the covert contact lenses wearer to adjust the distance desired so that the optimum desired supervision is achieved. Someday, soon, the covert contact lenses will adjust without the remote control device. This is a cool spy device that can be used without the suspect knowing that the covert contact lenses wearer is wearing the covert contact lenses because this is only known by limited people with top secret clearance. Now, you know how it feels to have top secret information and not be able to share it with your family or friends or even enemies.

Chapter 2 the Halloween Planner Company

It was a dark and stormy night with thunder and lightning, so I, Titus Uno Certified Public Accountant, Forensic Certified Public Accountant, Chartered Global Management Accountant, had just settled into my recliner to relax and watch the television. My eyes had just shut when there was a wrap at the door. I was startled at first, but I managed to get to the door before the person at the door could knock again. I opened the door. There stood a short old man with long hair. He was wearing a jogging suit and had a cane. When I saw his face, he had a patch over his left eye. He looked at me and asked me, "I am "Patch" MacGoo, are you Mr. Titus Uno?" I answer "Patch" MacGoo, "Yes l am Titus Uno Certified Public Accountant, Forensic Certified Public Accountant, Chartered Global Management Accountant, please come on in out of the rain." As "Patch" MacGoo entered he replied, "I thought that you were. That means that I am in the correct place."

After we had both sat down, "Patch" MacGoo told me that he had heard great things about me and my three Forensic Certified Public Accountant team members: Drew Samson – the private investigator, Dena Hope – the computer programmer and hacker, Veronica Jackson – the scheduler, organizer, and item collector. "Patch" MacGoo continued by saying that he was there representing the Halloween Planner Company. The Halloween Planner Company is a Global Halloween Planner Company, because the Halloween Planner Company ships Halloween items all over the world.

The Halloween Planner Company is located in Los Angeles, California, United States of America. That is where the movie stars are. My four Forensic Certified Public Accountant team and I will have a great time in Los Angeles, California, United States of America. By the way since, *The Forensic Certified Public Accountant and the Cremated of 64-SQUARES Financial Statements*, Jack "Sheriff" Starr, the Former 64-SQUARES CEO or the Former 64-SQUARES Chief Executive Officer, is now the CEO or Chief Executive Officer of my Forensic Certified Public Accountant team. I decided that Jack "Sheriff" Starr would be a great addition to the team. Jack "Sheriff" Starr makes my Forensic Certified Public Accountant team, 5 members, including myself. Jack "Sheriff" Starr said, "It is like a five-pointed star, and I am the sheriff."

Just to refresh your memory, Jack Starr is a very happily married man. His wife is Jessica Starr. Jack and Jessica are happily married and have been married for Twenty-three wonderful years. They have 5 children: two boys, Jim Starr and Jeff Starr and 3 girls, Janet Starr, Jill Starr, and Joan Starr. Jack and Jessica, Jim, Jeff, Janet, Jill, and Joan Starr all get along with each other and the have fun spending time with each other. They always take an annual family vacation. Over the years they have been to Paris, London, Hawaii, Orlando, Rome, Sydney, Cairo, Rio, Tokyo, Toronto, New York, and Washington, D.C. Jack Starr believes that spending time with his family is his favorite thing to do when he is not working or when he is not watching western movies. I thought that you would like to know that Jack Starr found work with my Forensic Certified Public Accountant team. Now he says, "Who is the sheriff of Titus Uno, CPA FCPA CGMA's team?" We always answer, "You are Jack Starr. You are Jack "Sheriff" Starr."

"Patch" MacGoo continued to say that he was there representing the Halloween Planner Company. Sorry about that, I decided to back up to get back on track. That is when "Patch" MacGoo got the strangest look of his face. His face was white as a sheet. The way he looked sent a chill down my back.

"Patch" MacGoo told me that the Halloween Planner Company has an Account Manager of the Halloween Planner Company, "Orange" Pumpkin, in Los Angeles, California, United States of America. The local Halloween Planner Company Account Manager usually checks on the repeat customers for their Halloween events. However, this year when "Orange" Pumpkin checked on the Trick-or-Treating accounts, the Halloween Candies accounts, the Halloween Costumes accounts, the Haunted Houses accounts, the Halloween Decorations accounts, the Halloween Parties accounts, the Halloween Dances accounts, the Halloween Movies accounts, The Halloween Cards accounts, the Halloween Mazes accounts, and the Jack-O-Lanterns and Pumpkin Patches accounts, "Orange" Pumpkin found out the Halloween orders had already been set up by "Orange" Pumpkin and all of the Halloween Orders had been "Paid-in-Full."

"Orange" Pumpkin has not talked with any of their customers and has not sent out any invoices to their customers either. "Orange" Pumpkin is worried that she may be the victim of identity theft or that there is a ghost employee. A "ghost employee" is an employee that gets a paycheck, but does not actually work there. It is as if the person is made up or fictitious. The main goal is to cheat the business out of salary monies by collecting the money for the "ghost employee" that is not really there, but the business think that the "ghost employee" is still there. How funny a ghost employee at Halloween.

The "ghost employee" can do what they want to because they are not there, but things get done so that the "ghost employee" or the one that gets the money can actually get the money. If it is a real or actual employee that gets the "ghost employee's" paycheck or money it is as if the real or actual employee is getting two paychecks. In this case, the "ghost employee" actually performed the work as "Orange" Pumpkin which is as discussed earlier as "identity theft." The fake invoice was paid by the purchaser of the Halloween Planner Company, but sent to the wrong address. So this action is actually identity theft ghost employee stealing money out of the Halloween Planner Company Headquarters pockets.

"Patch" MacGoo told me, Titus Uno, Certified Public Accountant, Forensic Certified Public Accountant, Chartered Global Management Accountant that the Halloween Planner Company was very interest in hiring my five member Forensic Certified Public Accountant team to help them find the Identity Theft Ghost Employee.

It was time to round up my five member Forensic Certified Public Accountant team: Drew Samson – the private investigator, Dena Hope – the computer programmer and hacker, Veronica Jackson – the scheduler, organizer, and item collector, Jack "Sheriff" Starr- CEO or Chief Executive Office, and myself, Titus Uno, Certified Public Accountant, Forensic Certified Public Accountant, Chartered Global Management Accountant. It is time to get to work to see if we can help the Halloween Planner Company with the Halloween Planner Company Headquarters "identity theft ghost employee" issue.

After we packed our bags, my five member Forensic Certified Public Accountant team, including myself, were accompanied by "Patch" MacGoo. We were in the Halloween Planner Company Headquarters private jet plane and were on our way to Los Angeles, California, United States of America. While we were on the jet plane, we developed our game plan and each member got their assignments to start this case. We will start with the Halloween Planner Company Headquarters and meet the Halloween Planner Company Headquarters employees.

All of the employees are very friendly and happy. If the employee sees or meets someone else, the employees always speak to each other. They do not ask each other, "How are you doing?" and just walk off without hearing the other person. It makes me smile to see people take a moment to be nice or friendly to each other. It is easy to see that this is a great place to work.

The employees are ready to get this problem of, the "identity theft ghost employee" solved, so that the Halloween Planner Company can move on and concentrate on the hard and very busy work of planning and executing the plan to perfection so that the Halloween Planner Company Headquarters client is not even aware the employees are there except the fact that some of the workers are servers and are visible.

There are 100 full time the Halloween Planner Company Headquarter workers. During the Halloween Season the Halloween Planner Company Headquarter hires about 250 Halloween seasonal workers. Each and every seasonal worker works everyday getting ready for the Halloween event and every night working the actual Halloween event. Every Day in October is filled with Halloween events.

The Halloween Planner Company has planned for October for the entire year. It takes that planning because the Halloween Planner Company is a professional Halloween Planner Company for any event that has to do with Halloween. The Halloween Planner Company is a well-oiled machine, until someone messes with the well-oiled machine. My five member Forensic Certified Public Accountant team: Drew Samson – the private investigator, Dena Hope – the computer programmer and hacker, Veronica Jackson – the scheduler, organizer, and item collector, Jack "Sheriff" Starr- CEO or Chief Executive Office, and myself.

The Halloween Planner Company has great Officer that oversees the operations of The Halloween Planner Company Headquarter Divisions: Halloween inventory storage building where all of the Halloween decorations such as: the Halloween Trick-or-Treating items, the Halloween Candies are stored in the coolers, the Halloween Costumes, the Haunted House or Haunted Mansion items, the Halloween Decorations for homes and businesses, the Halloween Parties favors and decorations, the Halloween Dances items and decorations, the Halloween Movies decorations and equipment, the Halloween Cards and envelopes, the Halloween Mazes items, and the Jack-O-Lanterns and pumpkin patches items and decorations are stored.

The CEO or the Chief Executive Officer of the Halloween Planner Company is Autumn Fall who has worked for the Halloween Planner Company for 6 years. Autumn Fall and Spring Summer are best friends and have been since they met each other in kindergarten. People are always amazed at how well they get along. They have never had a personal disagreement.

Autumn Fall, the CEO or the Chief Executive Officer of the Halloween Planner Company is married to Guy Fall. Guy and Autumn have a son, Skywalker Fall, who is 7years old. The Fall family has fun traveling to beach by the ocean.

The CFO or the Chief Financial Officer of the Halloween Planner Company is Spring Summer who has worked for the Halloween Planner Company for 5 years. These pair of officers, Spring Summer and Autumn Fall, combine to make the Halloween Planner Company Headquarters fiscal year financial statements look better each year because they have repeat clients and new clients. Each year the repeat clients want more and more. The bigger it gets the more the clients enjoy their activity. If someone just stands there and watches the activities, there is a great chance that that person is amazed at everything that is going on around that person. The Halloween Planner Company plans the best Halloween activities.

Spring Summer, the CFO or the Chief Financial Officer of the Halloween Planner Company is married to her husband, Butch Summer. Butch and Spring have a son, Gold Summer, who is 9 years old and a daughter, Silver Summer, who is 7years old.

Titus Uno, Certified Public Accountant, Forensic Certified Public Accountant, and Chartered Global Management Accountant and the Forensic Certified Public Accountant team: Drew Samson, Dena Hope, Jack "Sheriff" Starr, and Veronica Jackson must investigate the Halloween Planner Company Headquarters.

Drew Samson used his Private Investigators experience and high-technology gadgets to gain information on the Halloween Planner Company Headquarters. Drew Samson used the "blood-hound" to track down the 18 wheeler truck. Drew Samson uses the most high technology available such as: cameras to take pictures, drones to take videos, cell phones to communicate, Global Positioning System chips to track where suspects travel, night vision binoculars that deer hunters use and supersonic listening devices like those used at football games, ear piece combined with shades recorders to communicate with each other, polygraph machines to get to the truth, and wiretaps to gather information about the company, its employees to make it possible to reconstruct the financials and to help assist in the prosecution of the crime. This high technology is exciting to use because spying on people is fun to gain information on the Halloween Planner Company Headquarters.

Dena Hope uses her programming skills and hacking skills to get information about the Halloween Planner Company so the Dena Hope can investigate the Halloween Planner Company Headquarters. Dena Hope has at her disposal a high-technology van that is an undercover vehicle. This way she can move around Los Angeles, California, United States of America.

Jack "Sheriff" Starr, the CEO of the Forensic Certified Public Accountant team, helps the other team members if the other team members need someone else to help them because sometimes it is impossible for one person to complete the task alone. Jack "Sheriff" Starr used his charismatic personality to get other people to talk to him and to get things accomplished. He uses his cowboy charm to investigate the Halloween Planner Company Headquarters.

Veronica Jackson set up a times for the Forensic Certified Public Accountant team members so that can meet with the employees to investigate the Halloween Planner Company Headquarters. Veronica Jackson uses her connections to get the Forensic Certified Public

Accountant team into see very important people and to get the team special items such as high-technology gadgets that might be needed during the case.

I, Titus Uno, Certified Public Accountant, Forensic Certified Public Accountant, and Chartered Global Management Accountant, will have to investigate the Halloween Planner Company Headquarters with the help of my Forensic Certified Public Accountant team: Drew Samson, Dena Hope, Jack "Sheriff" Starr, and Veronica Jackson. I, Titus Uno, Certified Public Accountant, Forensic Certified Public Accountant, and Chartered Global Management Accountant, could not be a lay witness without their help. Thank you, Drew Samson, Dena Hope, Jack "Sheriff" Starr, and Veronica Jackson.

Chapter 4 the Halloween Planner Company Halloween Inventory Storage Building

The Halloween Planner Company Headquarters has a Halloween inventory storage building where all of the Halloween decorations such as: the Halloween Trick-or-Treating items, the Halloween Candies are stored in the coolers, the Halloween Costumes, the Haunted House or Haunted Mansion items, the Halloween Decorations for homes and businesses, the Halloween Parties favors and decorations, the Halloween Dances items and decorations, the Halloween Movies decorations and equipment, the Halloween Cards and envelopes, the Halloween Mazes items, and the Jack-O-Lanterns and pumpkin patches items and decorations are stored.

The "identity theft ghost employee" must be a professional thief because whoever setup all of the Halloween Planner Company Headquarters clients activities slipped into the Halloween Planner Company Headquarters' Halloween inventory storage building as if the "identity theft ghost employee" knew how to carry out covert operations. The "identity theft ghost employee" bypassed the Halloween Planner Company Headquarters' security system without the system alerting the Los Angeles Police Department or the LAPD. The Halloween Planner Company Headquarters' security system was the first thing that Drew Samson, the private investigator of my Forensic Certified Public Accountant team, looked at to try to get an understanding of the skills that the "identity theft ghost employee" must possess in order to get passed this security system. The "identity theft ghost employee" must possess some great skills because the Halloween Planner Company Headquarters security system is the DDT5000 secret security system. Only about a thousand people even know about how this security system works. The

DDT5000 secret security system was developed by the collaboration of professional burglars from all over the world. These professional burglars told the designer that this system could never ever be bypassed. In fact, after an afternoon of research, Drew Samson, the private investigator of my Forensic Certified Public Accountant team, found out that the "identity theft ghost employee" has been the one and only burglar to ever disable and get past the backup alarm of the DDT5000 secret security system. This is was you would say is a very important piece of information. The "identity theft ghost employee" must be a professional burglar with the very best burglary knowledge and skills that are necessary to get past the world's best security system, the DDT5000 secret security system.

Drew Samson, the private investigator of my Forensic Certified Public Accountant team, proceeded to try to recreate what the "identity theft ghost employee" must have done to get the Halloween Planner Company Headquarters' inventory out of the Halloween inventory storage building. He starts by looking for the obvious things that are there that should not be there, and for things that are there that should be there.

As Drew Samson, the private investigator of my Forensic Certified Public Accountant team, scans the Halloween Planner Company Headquarters' Halloween inventory storage building, how did some of the large pieces of decorations get removed without being detected by the security guards and the security guard dogs? There were some scratch mark that were on the floor that led to the 18-wheeler truck loading dock. Drew Samson, the private investigator of my Forensic Certified Public Accountant team, deduced that these scrapes were made by the "identity theft ghost employee" because these scrapes were made by someone that was in a hurry.

This is when Drew Samson, the private investigator of my Forensic Certified Public Accountant team, begins to smile because this is where the high-technology electronic "blood-hounds" are brought out. The ""blood-hounds" are a device that scans an item into its system and it can track down where the items has been. In this case, Drew Samson, the private investigator of my Forensic Certified Public Accountant team, can scan into the "blood-hounds" then the tracking begins. Drew Samson looks at the tire tracks and chooses the tracks that were left by an 18-wheeler truck that left in a hurry and a left darker track than all the other tracks. The "blood-hounds" tell Drew when the tracks turn left or right.

The "blood-hounds" performed just like Drew Samson had hoped. Technology is great. Drew Samson was looking at the 18-wheeler that was used in the theft of the Halloween Planner Company Headquarters' Halloween inventory. Drew Samson peeked into the cab of the truck so see if there was any incriminating evidence that could be used to place that this 18-wheeler had indeed been used by the "identity theft ghost employee." As Drew Samson looked into the cab of the 18-wheeler he gave a big laugh because believe it or not there were Halloween candy wrappers all over the front seat and floorboard of the 18-wheeler truck. That is enough evidence, that Drew Samson called his discovery of this guilty 18-wheeler truck into the Los Angeles Police Department or the LAPD. Drew Samson is still smiling because this had been a great day.

Titus Uno, Certified Public Accountant, Forensic Certified Public Accountant, and Chartered Global Management Accountant and the Forensic Certified Public Accountant team: Drew Samson, Dena Hope, Jack "Sheriff" Starr, and Veronica Jackson must investigate the Halloween Planner Company Headquarters Halloween inventory storage building.

Drew Samson used his Private Investigators experience and his high-technology gadgets to gain information on the Halloween Planner Company Headquarters' Halloween inventory storage building. Drew Samson used the "blood-hound" to track down the 18 wheeler truck. Drew Samson uses the most high technology available such as: cameras to take pictures, drones to take videos, cell phones to communicate, Global Positioning System chips to track where suspects travel, night vision binoculars that deer hunters use and supersonic listening devices like those used at football games, ear piece combined with shades recorders to communicate with each other, polygraph machines to get to the truth, and wiretaps to gather information about the company, its employees to make it possible to reconstruct the financials and to help assist in the prosecution of the crime. This high technology is exciting to use because spying on people is fun to gain information on the Halloween Planner Company Headquarters' Halloween inventory storage building.

Dena Hope uses her programming skills and hacking skills to get information about the Halloween Planner Company so the Dena Hope can investigate the Halloween Planner Company Headquarters' Halloween inventory storage building. Dena Hope has at her disposal a high-technology van that is an undercover vehicle. This way she can move around Los Angeles, California, United States of America.

Jack "Sheriff" Starr, the CEO of the Forensic Certified Public Accountant team, helps the other team members if the other team members need someone else to help them because sometimes it is impossible for one person to complete the task alone. Jack "Sheriff" Starr used his charismatic personality to get other people to talk to him and to get things accomplished. He uses his cowboy charm to investigate the Halloween Planner Company Headquarters' Halloween inventory storage building.

Veronica Jackson set up a times for the Forensic Certified Public Accountant team members so that can meet with the employees to investigate the Halloween Planner Company Headquarters' Halloween inventory storage building. Veronica Jackson uses her connections to get the Forensic Certified Public Accountant team into see very important people and to get the team special items such as high-technology gadgets that might be needed during the case.

I, Titus Uno, Certified Public Accountant, Forensic Certified Public Accountant, and Chartered Global Management Accountant, will have to investigate the Halloween Planner Company Headquarters' Halloween inventory storage building with the help of my Forensic Certified Public Accountant team: Drew Samson, Dena Hope, Jack "Sheriff" Starr, and Veronica Jackson. I, Titus Uno, Certified Public Accountant, Forensic Certified Public Accountant, and Chartered Global Management Accountant, could not be a lay witness without their help. Thank you, Drew Samson, Dena Hope, Jack "Sheriff" Starr, and Veronica Jackson.

"Orange" Pumpkin called to check on the Halloween Planner Company Headquarters "Trick-or –Treat" Accounts, but to her surprise the "Trick-or –Treat" account had already been completed and the account had already been sent to another address. This is a nightmare for any company. There is not any companies that wants to have their profits stolen. This is why me, Titus Uno, Certified Public Accountant, Forensic Certified Public Accountant, and Chartered Global Management Accountant, and my team are on the job to investigate the Halloween Planner Company Headquarters Halloween "Trick or Treat" Division.

"Trick or Treat" is a phrase that every child know how to say. This is the number one type of account that the Halloween Planner Company plans or caters the event for their clients. The children dressed in their costumes that was bought at the Halloween Planner Company run up to the house front door and rings the bell and waits for the people in the house to open the door. The children shout, "Trick or Treat." The homeowner gives the children candy that they bought at the Halloween Planner Company in the children's Halloween sack that was also bought at the Halloween Planner Company.

The Halloween Planner Company offers clients different packages for the client's "Trick or Treat." The Halloween Planner Company can deliver the candy. Decorations can be added for a larger package option. Fog machines makes an even larger package. Halloween music makes a great option to add to the package. The Halloween Planner Company offers anything that is Halloween available to their clients. I, Titus Uno, Certified Public Accountant, Forensic Certified Public Accountant, Forensic Certified Public Accountant, believe that if one of their clients wanted an orange Christmas tree that the Halloween Planner Company would make it happen. After all the Halloween Planner Company is the best Halloween Planner Company that there is in the whole word.

The Halloween Planner Company offers a variety of Halloween "Trick-or-Treat" decorations themes: Movie themes "Trick-or-Treat", Television Themes "Trick-or-Treat", Spider webs themes "Trick-or-Treat", Ghost themes "Trick-or-Treat", Mad Scientist themes "Trick-or-Treat", Frankenstein themes "Trick-or-Treat", Werewolf themes "Trick-or-Treat", Dracula theme "Trick-or-Treat", and many more choices.

Movie themes "Trick-or-Treat" where the people are dress up in costumes as Movie characters. This gives the "Trick-or-Treaters" the feeling that they are seeing characters from the Movie or Movies. The "Trick-or-Treaters" say, "Trick-or-Treat." Then the "Trick-or-Treater" grabs the candy. Movies play candy ads before movies start.

Television themes "Trick-or-Treat" are where the people handing out the candies are the people moving around are dressed as Television characters. They hand the candies to the "Trick-or-Treater.". Television ads are import in the candy business.

Spider webs themes "Trick-or-Treat" are part of the scene where fake spider webs are hung all around the area that the candies are handed out to the "Trick-or-Treater.". Spiders often have happy cute faces and soft bodies with their legs.

Ghost themes "Trick-or-Treat" has the scene filled with friendly and unfriendly ghosts that are flying around as "Trick-or-Treater" get their treats. Some ghosts are very friendly.

Mad Scientist themes "Trick-or-Treat" is popular because the Mad Scientist labs are made with beakers and flasks, and flashing lights all over the place as the "Trick-or-Treater" get their treats. Mar Scientists like to wear their white lab coats.

Frankenstein themes "Trick-or-Treat" is popular because Frankenstein is on the table where he comes to life as the "Trick-or-Treater" get their treats. Frankenstein has bolts sticking out of his neck.

Werewolf themes "Trick-or-Treat" is where the Werewolf is howling with the moon behind the moon as the "Trick-or-Treater" get their treats. Werewolves are cures with growing lots of hair when there is a full moon.

Dracula theme "Trick-or-Treat" is usually with Dracula posing with his arm and cape covering the bottom of his face and his fangs as the "Trick-or-Treater" get their treats. Dracula sleeps in coffins. Enough said.

Titus Uno, Certified Public Accountant, Forensic Certified Public Accountant, and Chartered Global Management Accountant and the Forensic Certified Public Accountant team: Drew Samson, Dena Hope, Jack "Sheriff" Starr, and Veronica Jackson must investigate the Halloween Planner Company Headquarters Halloween "Trick or Treat" Division.

Drew Samson used his Private Investigators experience to gain information on the Halloween Planner Company "Trick or Treat" Division. Drew Samson uses the most high technology available such as: cameras to take pictures, drones to take videos, cell phones to communicate, Global Positioning System chips to track where suspects travel, night vision binoculars that deer hunters use and supersonic listening devices like those used at football games, ear piece combined with shades recorders to communicate with each other, polygraph machines to get to the truth, and wiretaps to gather information about the company, its employees to make it possible to reconstruct the financials and to help assist in the prosecution of the crime. This high technology is exciting to use because spying on people is fun to gain information on the Halloween Planner Company Headquarters' Halloween "Trick-or-Treating" division.

Dena Hope uses her programming skills and hacking skills to get information about the Halloween Planner Company so the Dena Hope can investigate the Halloween Planner Company Headquarters' Halloween "Trick or Treat" Division. Dena Hope has at her disposal a high-technology van that is an undercover vehicle. This way she can move around Los Angeles, California, United States of America.

Dena Hope uses her programming skills and hacking skills to get information about the Halloween Planner Company so the Dena Hope can investigate the Halloween Planner Company "Trick or Treat" division.

Jack "Sheriff" Starr, the CEO of the Forensic Certified Public Accountant team, helps the other team members if the other team members need someone else to help them because sometimes it is impossible for one person to complete the task alone. Jack "Sheriff" Starr used his charismatic personality to get other people to talk to him and to get things accomplished. He uses his cowboy charm to investigate the Halloween Planner Company Headquarters' Halloween "Trick or Treat" division.

Veronica Jackson set up a times for the Forensic Certified Public Accountant team members so that can meet with the employees to investigate the Halloween Planner Company Headquarters' Halloween "Trick or Treat" division. Veronica Jackson uses her connections to get the Forensic Certified Public Accountant team into see very important people and to get the team special items such as high-technology gadgets that might be needed during the case.

I, Titus Uno, Certified Public Accountant, Forensic Certified Public Accountant, and Chartered Global Management Accountant, will have to investigate the Halloween Planner Company "Trick or Treat" division with the help of my Forensic Certified Public Accountant team: Drew Samson, Dena Hope, Jack "Sheriff" Starr, and Veronica Jackson. I, Titus Uno,

Certified Public Accountant, Forensic Certified Public Accountant, and Chartered Global Management Accountant, could not be a lay witness without their help. Thank you, Drew Samson, Dena Hope, Jack "Sheriff" Starr, and Veronica Jackson.

"Orange" Pumpkin called to check on the Halloween Planner Company Headquarters Candies Accounts, but to her surprise the Candies account had already been completed and the account had already been sent to another address. This is a nightmare for any company. There is not any companies that wants to have their profits stolen. This is why I, Titus Uno, Certified Public Accountant, Forensic Certified Public Accountant, and Chartered Global Management Accountant, and my team are on the job to investigate the Halloween Planner Company Headquarters Halloween Candies Division.

The Halloween Planner Company has a delivery service for clients to have the Halloween Planner Company to deliver candies to the clients to hand out to the children as described earlier. If the client runs out the Halloween Planner Company can deliver more.

Candy, candy, candy everywhere. Candy and Halloween go together at this time of year. There are soft candies, hard candies, chocolates, licorice, candy bars, and many more types of candy that are sealed separately. This makes the candy to stay fresher longer.

The Halloween Planner Company sells candies to clients because candy is an important part of Halloween. Chocolate candy bars are the number one selling candy that the Halloween Planner Company sells.

The Halloween Planner Company offers a variety of Halloween Candies themes: Movie themes "Trick-or-Treat", Television themes "Trick-or-Treat", Spider webs themes "Trick-or-Treat", Ghost themes "Trick-or-Treat", Mad Scientist themes "Trick-or-Treat", Frankenstein themes "Trick-or-Treat", Werewolf themes "Trick-or-Treat", Dracula theme "Trick-or-Treat", and many more choices.

Movie Candies themes where the people are dress up in costumes as Movie characters. This gives the "Trick-or-Treaters" the feeling that they are seeing characters from the Movie or Movies. The "Trick-or-Treaters" say, "Trick-or-Treat." Then the "Trick-or-Treater" grabs the candy. Movies show candy in the movies. Everyone has their favorite movie candies.

Television Candies themes are where the people handing out the candies are the people moving around are dressed as Television characters. They hand the candies to the "Trick-or-Treater." What candies do you purchase to eat when you go to the couch or to your favorite chair to watch your favorite television shows?

Spider webs Candies themes are part of the scene where fake spider webs are hung all around the area that the candies are handed out to the "Trick-or-Treater." Spiders have 8 legs.

Ghost Candies themes has the scene filled with friendly and unfriendly ghosts that are flying around as the "Trick-or-Treater" get their treats. Ghosts usually have unfinished work to finish here on earth.

Mad Scientist Candies themes is popular because the Mad Scientist labs are made with beakers and flasks, and flashing lights all over the place as the "Trick-or-Treater" get their treats. Mad Scientists usually wear their goggles.

Frankenstein Candies themes is popular because Frankenstein is on the table where he comes to life as the "Trick-or-Treater" get their treats. Frankenstein has a large square head and a flat-top hair cut.

Werewolf Candies themes is where the Werewolf is howling with the moon behind the moon as the "Trick-or-Treater" get their treats. Werewolves change back into human form when the full moon goes behind nighttime clouds.

Dracula Candies themes is usually with Dracula posing with his arm and cape covering the bottom of his face and his fangs as the "Trick-or-Treater" get their treats. Dracula loves to eat cereal.

Titus Uno, Certified Public Accountant, Forensic Certified Public Accountant, and Chartered Global Management Accountant and the Forensic Certified Public Accountant team: Drew Samson, Dena Hope, Jack "Sheriff" Starr, and Veronica Jackson must investigate the Halloween Planner Company Headquarters' Halloween Candies Division.

Drew Samson used his Private Investigators experience and his high-technology gadgets to gain information on the Halloween Planner Company Headquarters' Halloween Candies division. Drew Samson uses the most high technology available such as: cameras to take pictures, drones to take videos, cell phones to communicate, Global Positioning System chips to track where suspects travel, night vision binoculars that deer hunters use and supersonic listening devices like those used at football games, ear piece combined with shades recorders to communicate with each other, polygraph machines to get to the truth, and wiretaps to gather information about the company, its employees to make it possible to reconstruct the financials and to help assist in the prosecution of the crime. This high technology is exciting to use because spying on people is fun to gain information on the Halloween Planner Company Headquarters' Halloween Candies Division.

Dena Hope uses her programming skills and hacking skills to get information about the Halloween Planner Company so the Dena Hope can investigate the Halloween Planner Company

Headquarters' Halloween Candies Division. Dena Hope has at her disposal a high-technology van that is an undercover vehicle. This way she can move around Los Angeles, California, United States of America.

Dena Hope uses her programming skills and hacking skills to get information about the Halloween Planner Company so the Dena Hope can investigate the Halloween Planner Company Headquarters' Halloween Candies division.

Jack "Sheriff" Starr, the CEO of the Forensic Certified Public Accountant team, helps the other team members if the other team members need someone else to help them because sometimes it is impossible for one person to complete the task alone. Jack "Sheriff" Starr used his charismatic personality to get other people to talk to him and to get things accomplished. He uses his cowboy charm to investigate the Halloween Planner Company Headquarters' Halloween Candies Division.

Veronica Jackson set up a times for the Forensic Certified Public Accountant team members so that can meet with the employees to investigate the Halloween Planner Company Headquarters' Halloween Candies Division. Veronica Jackson uses her connections to get the Forensic Certified Public Accountant team into see very important people and to get the team special items such as high-technology gadgets that might be needed during the case.

I, Titus Uno, Certified Public Accountant, Forensic Certified Public Accountant, and Chartered Global Management Accountant, will have to investigate the Halloween Planner Company Headquarters' Halloween Candies Division with the help of my Forensic Certified Public Accountant team: Drew Samson, Dena Hope, Jack "Sheriff" Starr, and Veronica Jackson. I, Titus Uno, Certified Public Accountant, Forensic Certified Public Accountant, and Chartered

Global Management Accountant, could not be a lay witness without their help. Thank you, Drew Samson, Dena Hope, Jack "Sheriff" Starr, and Veronica Jackson.

"Orange" Pumpkin called to check on the Halloween Planner Company Headquarters costumes Accounts, but to her surprise the Costumes account had already been completed and the account had already been sent to another address. This is a nightmare for any company. There is not any companies that wants to have their profits stolen. This is why I, Titus Uno, Certified Public Accountant, Forensic Certified Public Accountant, and Chartered Global Management Accountant, and my team are on the job to investigate the Halloween Planner Company Headquarters Halloween Costumes Division.

The Halloween Planner Company offers a variety of costumes to clients. At Halloween, people are always looking for costumes to wear to all the events that are listed, described, and explained below.

The Halloween Planner Company offers a variety of Halloween Costume themes: Movie Costume themes, Television Costume themes, Spider webs Costume themes, Ghost Costume themes, Mad Scientist Costume themes, Frankenstein Costume themes, Werewolf Costume themes, Dracula Costume themes, and many more themes.

Movie Costume themes where there is usually with Dracula posing with his arm and cape covering the bottom of his face and his fangs as the "Trick-or-Treater" get their treats. People love to pretend to pretend to be their favorite television stars or actors.

Television Costume themes are where the people handing out the candies are the people moving around are dressed as Television characters. They hand the candies to the "Trick-or-Treater." People love to pretend to pretend to be their favorite television stars or actors.

Spider webs Costume themes are part of the scene where fake spider webs are hung all around the area that the candies are handed out to the "Trick-or-Treater." Spiders love to spin their webs to catch their prey.

Ghost Costume themes has the scene filled with friendly and unfriendly ghosts that are flying around as the "Trick-or-Treater" get their treats. Ghosts are translucent to humans.

Mad Scientist Costume themes is popular because the Mad Scientist labs are made with beakers and flasks, and flashing lights all over the place as the "Trick-or-Treater" get their treats. Mad Scientists want to rule the world.

Frankenstein Costume themes is popular because Frankenstein is on the table where he comes to life as the "Trick-or-Treater" get their treats. Frankenstein is very tall and very big.

Werewolf Costume themes is where the Werewolf is howling with the moon behind the moon as the "Trick-or-Treater" get their treats. Werewolves turn inter Werewolves when there is a full moon.

Dracula Costume themes is usually with Dracula posing with his arm and cape covering the bottom of his face and his fangs as the "Trick-or-Treater" get their treats. Dracula is known for turning into a bat.

Titus Uno, Certified Public Accountant, Forensic Certified Public Accountant, and Chartered Global Management Accountant and the Forensic Certified Public Accountant team: Drew Samson, Dena Hope, Jack "Sheriff" Starr, and Veronica Jackson must investigate the Halloween Planner Company Headquarters Halloween Costumes Division.

Drew Samson used his Private Investigators experience and his high-technology gadgets o gain information on the Halloween Planner Company Headquarters' Halloween Costumes

Division.   Drew Samson uses the most high technology available such as: cameras to take pictures, drones to take videos, cell phones to communicate, Global Positioning System chips to track where suspects travel, night vision binoculars that deer hunters use and supersonic listening devices like those used at football games, ear piece combined with shades recorders to communicate with each other, polygraph machines to get to the truth, and wiretaps to gather information about the company, its employees to make it possible to reconstruct the financials and to help assist in the prosecution of the crime. This high technology is exciting to use because spying on people is fun to gain information on the Halloween Planner Company Headquarters' Halloween Costume Division.

Dena Hope uses her programming skills and hacking skills to get information about the Halloween Planner Company so the Dena Hope can investigate the Halloween Planner Company Headquarters' Halloween Costume Division. Dena Hope has at her disposal a high-technology van that is an undercover vehicle. This way she can move around Los Angeles, California, United States of America.

Dena Hope uses her programming skills and hacking skills to get information about the Halloween Planner Company so the Dena Hope can investigate the Halloween Planner Company Headquarters' Halloween Costumes Division.

Jack "Sheriff" Starr, the CEO of the Forensic Certified Public Accountant team, helps the other team members if the other team members need someone else to help them because sometimes it is impossible for one person to complete the task alone. Jack "Sheriff" Starr used his charismatic personality to get other people to talk to him and to get things accomplished. He uses his cowboy charm to investigate the Halloween Planner Company Headquarters' Halloween Costumes Division.

Veronica Jackson set up a times for the Forensic Certified Public Accountant team members so that can meet with the employees to investigate the Halloween Planner Company Headquarters' Halloween Costumes Division. Veronica Jackson uses her connections to get the Forensic Certified Public Accountant team into see very important people and to get the team special items such as high-technology gadgets that might be needed during the case.

I, Titus Uno, Certified Public Accountant, Forensic Certified Public Accountant, and Chartered Global Management Accountant, will have to investigate the Halloween Planner Company Headquarters' Halloween Costumes Division with the help of my Forensic Certified Public Accountant team: Drew Samson, Dena Hope, Jack "Sheriff" Starr, and Veronica Jackson. I, Titus Uno, Certified Public Accountant, Forensic Certified Public Accountant, and Chartered Global Management Accountant, could not be a lay witness without their help. Thank you, Drew Samson, Dena Hope, Jack "Sheriff" Starr, and Veronica Jackson.

Chapter 8 Haunted Houses or Haunted Mansions Accounting for These Accounts

"Orange" Pumpkin called to check on the Halloween Planner Company Headquarters Haunted Houses or Haunted Mansions Accounting Accounts, but to her surprise the Haunted Houses or Haunted Mansions Accounting account had already been completed and the account had already been sent to another address. This is a nightmare for any company. There is not any companies that wants to have their profits stolen. This is why I, Titus Uno, Certified Public Accountant, Forensic Certified Public Accountant, and Chartered Global Management Accountant, and my team are on the job to investigate the Halloween Planner Company Headquarters' Halloween Haunted Houses or Haunted Mansions Accounting Division.

The Halloween Planner Company offers a variety of services to clients that are interested in setting up a Haunted House or a Haunted Mansion.

The Halloween Planner Company helps companies decorate their businesses, both inside and outside. Using the Halloween Planner Company gives the businesses a professional look for Halloween.

The Halloween Planner Company help decorate family homes and mansions both inside and outside. Using the Halloween Planner Company gives the home a professional look for Halloween. It is exciting to have Halloween decorations place at a house.

The Halloween Planner Company offers a variety of Halloween Haunted Houses or Haunted Mansions decorations themes: Movie Halloween Haunted Houses or Haunted Mansions decorations themes, Television Halloween Haunted Houses or Haunted Mansions decorations themes, Spider webs Halloween Haunted Houses or Haunted Mansions decorations themes, Ghost Halloween Haunted Houses or Haunted Mansions decorations themes, Mad Scientist Halloween Haunted Houses or Haunted Mansions decorations themes, Frankenstein Halloween Haunted Houses or Haunted Mansions decorations themes, Werewolf Halloween Haunted Houses or Haunted Mansions decorations themes, Dracula Halloween Haunted Houses or Haunted Mansions decorations themes, and many more Halloween Haunted Houses or Haunted Mansions decorations themes.

Movie themes Halloween Haunted Houses or Haunted Mansions is where the Halloween Planner Company goes into the Haunted Houses or Haunted Mansions and decorate the Haunted Houses or Haunted Mansions with Halloween decoration to their clients favorite movies. These are fun to decorate because the Haunted Houses or Haunted Mansions are in Los Angeles, California, United States of America.

Television Halloween Haunted Houses or Haunted Mansions themes is where the Halloween Planner Company goes into the Haunted Houses or Haunted Mansions and decorate the Haunted Houses or Haunted Mansions with Halloween decoration to their clients favorite television stars, actors or shows.

Spider webs Halloween Haunted Houses or Haunted Mansions themes are in every Haunted Houses or Haunted Mansions. These spider webs are very effective at making the Haunted Houses or Haunted Mansions very creepy and scary because that means that there is a spider and that there is no one to sweep them away. Not even a witch.

Ghost Halloween Haunted Houses or Haunted Mansions themes are where ghost fly around the Haunted Houses or Haunted Mansions and try to scare the occupants in the Haunted Houses or Haunted Mansions. Boo!

Mad Scientist Halloween Haunted Houses or Haunted Mansions themes usually have a lab in the basement of their Haunted Houses or Haunted Mansions. This lab is recreated by the Halloween Planner Company. This lab with all the crazy beakers and flasks laboratory recreating the experiments of the Mad Scientist.

Frankenstein Halloween Haunted Houses or Haunted Mansions themes is where the Frankenstein monster is placed in the laboratory where he is brought to life. The laboratory is set up by the Halloween Planner Company so that the laboratory really looks like it is actually a scene from a Halloween movie.

Werewolf Halloween Haunted Houses or Haunted Mansions themes is where that werewolf comes to life as it is transformed from human for into a werewolf. The werewolf howls at the fuel moon.

Dracula Halloween Haunted Houses or Haunted Mansions themes is where Dracula usually changes from human form to bat form and flies around then changes back into human form then changes again a from human form to bat form and flies around then changes back into human form then changes again from human form to bat form and flies around then changes back into human form then changes again from human form to bat form and flies around then changes back into human form…

Titus Uno, Certified Public Accountant, Forensic Certified Public Accountant, and Chartered Global Management Accountant and the Forensic Certified Public Accountant team: Drew

Samson, Dena Hope, Jack "Sheriff" Starr, and Veronica Jackson must investigate the Halloween Planner Company Headquarters Halloween Haunted Houses or Haunted Mansions Division.

Drew Samson used his Private Investigators experience to gain information on the Halloween Planner Company Headquarters' Halloween Haunted Houses or Haunted Mansions Division. Drew Samson uses the most high technology available such as: cameras to take pictures, drones to take videos, cell phones to communicate, Global Positioning System chips to track where suspects travel, night vision binoculars that deer hunters use and supersonic listening devices like those used at football games, ear piece combined with shades recorders to communicate with each other, polygraph machines to get to the truth, and wiretaps to gather information about the company, its employees to make it possible to reconstruct the financials and to help assist in the prosecution of the crime. This high technology is exciting to use because spying on people is fun to gain information on the Halloween Planner Company Headquarters' Halloween Haunted Houses or Haunted Mansions Divisions.

Dena Hope uses her programming skills and hacking skills to get information about the Halloween Planner Company so the Dena Hope can investigate the Halloween Planner Company Headquarters' Halloween Haunted Houses or Haunted Mansions Division. Dena Hope has at her disposal a high-technology van that is an undercover vehicle. This way she can move around Los Angeles, California, United States of America.

Dena Hope uses her programming skills and hacking skills to get information about the Halloween Planner Company so the Dena Hope can investigate the Halloween Planner Company Headquarters' Halloween Haunted Houses or Haunted Mansions Division.

Jack "Sheriff" Starr, the CEO of the Forensic Certified Public Accountant team, helps the other team members if the other team members need someone else to help them because

48

sometimes it is impossible for one person to complete the task alone. Jack "Sheriff" Starr used his charismatic personality to get other people to talk to him and to get things accomplished. He uses his cowboy charm to investigate the Halloween Planner Company Headquarters' Halloween inventory storage building.

Veronica Jackson set up a times for the Forensic Certified Public Accountant team members so that can meet with the employees to investigate the Halloween Planner Company Headquarters' Halloween inventory storage building. Veronica Jackson uses her connections to get the Forensic Certified Public Accountant team into see very important people and to get the team special items such as high-technology gadgets that might be needed during the case.

I, Titus Uno, Certified Public Accountant, Forensic Certified Public Accountant, and Chartered Global Management Accountant, will have to investigate the Halloween Planner Company Headquarters' Halloween Haunted Houses or Haunted Mansions Division with the help of my Forensic Certified Public Accountant team: Drew Samson, Dena Hope, Jack "Sheriff" Starr, and Veronica Jackson. I, Titus Uno, Certified Public Accountant, Forensic Certified Public Accountant, and Chartered Global Management Accountant, could not be a lay witness without their help. Thank you, Drew Samson, Dena Hope, Jack "Sheriff" Starr, and Veronica Jackson.

"Orange" Pumpkin called to check on the Halloween Planner Company Headquarters Decorations Accounts, but to her surprise the Decorations account had already been completed and the account had already been sent to another address. This is a nightmare for any company. There is not any companies that wants to have their profits stolen. This is why I, Titus Uno, Certified Public Accountant, Forensic Certified Public Accountant, and Chartered Global Management Accountant, and my team are on the job to investigate the Halloween Planner Company Headquarters Halloween Decorations Division.

The Halloween Planner Company offers a variety of Halloween decorations themes: Movie Halloween Decorations, Television Halloween Decorations, Spider webs Halloween Decorations, Ghost Halloween Decorations themes, Mad Scientist Halloween Decorations themes, Frankenstein themes Halloween Decorations themes, Werewolf Halloween Decorations themes, Dracula Halloween Decorations themes, send many more Halloween Decorations themes.

Movie Halloween Decorations themes is where the Halloween Planner Company offers items that allow their clients to recreate their favorite movie or movies. The clients choose their favorite movie or movies and the Halloween Planner Company puts together the decorations that makes that movie or movies come to life for their client.

Television Halloween Decorations themes is where the Halloween Planner Company offers items that allow their clients to recreate their favorite television shows. The clients choose their favorite television show or shows and the Halloween Planner Company puts together the decorations that makes that show or shows come to life for their client.

Spider webs Halloween Decorations themes is where the Halloween Planner Company offers items that allow their clients to recreate their favorite scene that has spider webs. The clients choose their favorite scene and the Halloween Planner Company puts together the decorations with spider webs everywhere that makes that show or shows come to life with spider webs for their client.

Ghost Halloween Decorations themes is where the Halloween Planner Company offers items that allow their clients to recreate their favorite scene that is filled with flying ghosts. The clients choose their favorite scene and the Halloween Planner Company puts together the decorations with ghosts that makes that show or shows come to life with ghosts flying for their client.

Mad Scientist Halloween Decorations themes is where the Halloween Planner Company offers items that allow their clients to recreate their scene that has the Mad Scientist hard at work to try to take over the world. The clients choose their favorite scene with the Mad Scientist's laboratory and the Halloween Planner Company puts together the decorations with Mad Scientist that makes that show or shows come to life with Mad Scientist experimenting for their client.

Frankenstein themes Halloween Decorations themes is where the Halloween Planner Company offers items that allow their clients to recreate their favorite Frankenstein scene that the client likes. The clients choose their favorite scene with the Frankenstein on the table in the laboratory and the Halloween Planner Company puts together the decorations with Frankenstein lying down on the table that makes that show or shows come to life with Frankenstein on the table for their client.

Werewolf Halloween Decorations themes is where the Halloween Planner Company offers items that allow their clients to recreate their favorite Werewolf scene sometime it involves the human changing into a werewolf in front of the Halloween visitors..

Dracula Halloween Decorations themes is where the Halloween Planner Company offers items that allow their clients to recreate their favorite Dracula scene. The clients choose their favorite scene with Dracula and the Halloween Planner Company puts together the decorations with Dracula that makes that show or shows come to life with Dracula for their client.

Titus Uno, Certified Public Accountant, Forensic Certified Public Accountant, and Chartered Global Management Accountant and the Forensic Certified Public Accountant team: Drew Samson, Dena Hope, Jack "Sheriff" Starr, and Veronica Jackson must investigate the Halloween Planner Company Headquarters' Halloween Decorations Division.

Drew Samson used his Private Investigators experience to gain information on the Halloween Planner Company Headquarters' Halloween Decorations Division.   Drew Samson uses the most high technology available such as: cameras to take pictures, drones to take videos, cell phones to communicate, Global Positioning System chips to track where suspects travel, night vision binoculars that deer hunters use and supersonic listening devices like those used at football games, ear piece combined with shades recorders to communicate with each other, polygraph machines to get to the truth, and wiretaps to gather information about the company, its employees to make it possible to reconstruct the financials and to help assist in the prosecution of the crime. This high technology is exciting to use because spying on people is fun to gain information on the Halloween Planner Company Headquarters' Halloween Decorations Division.

Dena Hope uses her programming skills and hacking skills to get information about the Halloween Planner Company so the Dena Hope can investigate the Halloween Planner Company

Headquarters' Halloween Decorations Division. Dena Hope has at her disposal a high-technology van that is an undercover vehicle. This way she can move around Los Angeles, California, United States of America.

Dena Hope uses her programming skills and hacking skills to get information about the Halloween Planner Company so the Dena Hope can investigate the Halloween Planner Company Headquarters' Halloween Decorations Division.

Jack "Sheriff" Starr, the CEO of the Forensic Certified Public Accountant team, helps the other team members if the other team members need someone else to help them because sometimes it is impossible for one person to complete the task alone. Jack "Sheriff" Starr used his charismatic personality to get other people to talk to him and to get things accomplished. He uses his cowboy charm to investigate the Halloween Planner Company Headquarters' Halloween Decorations Division.

Veronica Jackson set up a times for the Forensic Certified Public Accountant team members so that can meet with the employees to investigate the Halloween Planner Company Headquarters' Halloween Decorations Division. Veronica Jackson uses her connections to get the Forensic Certified Public Accountant team into see very important people and to get the team special items such as high-technology gadgets that might be needed during the case.

I, Titus Uno, Certified Public Accountant, Forensic Certified Public Accountant, and Chartered Global Management Accountant, will have to investigate the Halloween Planner Company Headquarters' Halloween Decorations Division with the help of my Forensic Certified Public Accountant team: Drew Samson, Dena Hope, Jack "Sheriff" Starr, and Veronica Jackson. I, Titus Uno, Certified Public Accountant, Forensic Certified Public Accountant, and Chartered

Global Management Accountant, could not be a lay witness without their help. Thank you,

Drew Samson, Dena Hope, Jack "Sheriff" Starr, and Veronica Jackson.

"Orange" Pumpkin called to check on the Halloween Planner Company Headquarters Parties Accounts, but to her surprise the Parties account had already been completed and the account had already been sent to another address. This is a nightmare for any company. There is not any companies that wants to have their profits stolen. This is why I, Titus Uno, Certified Public Accountant, Forensic Certified Public Accountant, and Chartered Global Management Accountant, and my team are on the job to investigate the Halloween Planner Company Headquarters Halloween Parties Division.

The Halloween Planner Company offers a variety of party packages to clients. Hayrides, Dunking for apples, Piñatas, Pumpkin Carving, Masquerade parties, Costumes parties, and several other party packages are available for the Halloween Planner Company clients to choose.

Hayrides are very fun to add to a party because party goers can relax on the back of a hayride and talk will relaxing. The sky makes a great view when the party goers look up at the night sky.

Dunking for apples is a fun game that party goers love to play during the Halloween Season that is why the Halloween Planner Company includes the Dunking for apples game.

Piñatas are a Halloween game that children, sometimes adults, love to play because you hit the piñata and Halloween candies fall out of the piñata. The Halloween Planner Company only puts Halloween candies into their piñatas.

Pumpkin Carving is very exciting Halloween activity for adults and teenagers to try during the Halloween Season. There are pumpkin carving pattern that can be used to make the pumpkins look like a professional pumpkin carver carved the pumpkin. Most people prefer carving the pumpkins freestyle.

Masquerade parties are exciting to plan according to the Halloween Planner Company. The party goers show up in their costumes, and then add their mask so that no one will know who the person is that they are talking to or visiting with. That is what it is a Masquerade party.

Costumes parties are just like Masquerade parties except masks are not worn. The people party and visit and have a great time. There are Halloween decorations setup all over the party area.

Titus Uno, Certified Public Accountant, Forensic Certified Public Accountant, and Chartered Global Management Accountant and the Forensic Certified Public Accountant team: Drew Samson, Dena Hope, Jack "Sheriff" Starr, and Veronica Jackson must investigate the Halloween Planner Company Headquarters' Halloween Parties Division.

Drew Samson used his Private Investigators experience to gain information on the Halloween Planner Company Headquarters' Halloween Parties Division. Drew Samson uses the most high technology available such as: cameras to take pictures, drones to take videos, cell phones to communicate, Global Positioning System chips to track where suspects travel, night vision binoculars that deer hunters use and supersonic listening devices like those used at football games, ear piece combined with shades recorders to communicate with each other, polygraph machines to get to the truth, and wiretaps to gather information about the company, its employees to make it possible to reconstruct the financials and to help assist in the prosecution of the crime. This high technology is exciting to use because spying on people is fun to gain information on the Halloween Planner Company Headquarters' Halloween Parties Division.

Dena Hope uses her programming skills and hacking skills to get information about the Halloween Planner Company so the Dena Hope can investigate the Halloween Planner Company Headquarters' Halloween Parties Division. Dena Hope has at her disposal a high-technology van that is an undercover vehicle. This way she can move around Los Angeles, California, United States of America.

Dena Hope uses her programming skills and hacking skills to get information about the Halloween Planner Company so the Dena Hope can investigate the Halloween Planner Company Headquarters' Halloween Parties Division.

Jack "Sheriff" Starr, the CEO of the Forensic Certified Public Accountant team, helps the other team members if the other team members need someone else to help them because sometimes it is impossible for one person to complete the task alone. Jack "Sheriff" Starr used his charismatic personality to get other people to talk to him and to get things accomplished. He uses his cowboy charm to investigate the Halloween Planner Company Headquarters' Halloween Parties Division.

Veronica Jackson set up a times for the Forensic Certified Public Accountant team members so that can meet with the employees to investigate the Halloween Planner Company Headquarters' Halloween Parties Division. Veronica Jackson uses her connections to get the Forensic Certified Public Accountant team into see very important people and to get the team special items such as high-technology gadgets that might be needed during the case.

I, Titus Uno, Certified Public Accountant, Forensic Certified Public Accountant, and Chartered Global Management Accountant, will have to investigate the Halloween Planner Company Headquarters' Halloween Parties Division with the help of my Forensic Certified Public Accountant team: Drew Samson, Dena Hope, Jack "Sheriff" Starr, and Veronica Jackson.

I, Titus Uno, Certified Public Accountant, Forensic Certified Public Accountant, and Chartered

Global Management Accountant, could not be a lay witness without their help. Thank you,

Drew Samson, Dena Hope, Jack "Sheriff" Starr, and Veronica Jackson.

"Orange" Pumpkin called to check on the Halloween Planner Company Headquarters Dances Accounts, but to her surprise the Dances account had already been completed and the account had already been sent to another address. This is a nightmare for any company. There is not any companies that wants to have their profits stolen. This is why I, Titus Uno, Certified Public Accountant, Forensic Certified Public Accountant, and Chartered Global Management Accountant, and my team are on the job to investigate the Halloween Planner Company Headquarters Halloween Dances Division.

The Halloween Planner Company offers a variety of Halloween Dances themes to clients: Costume Dances, Halloween masquerade dances with makes where the people dance, Halloween DJs or disc jockeys play music for the dance, Halloween bands can play for the Halloween dance, as well as other Halloween Dances themes.

Costume Dances are dances that the dancers at the Halloween Dance dress in costumes. These costumes can be any costume or the dance may have a specific theme such as Movies, television stars or shows, Halloween characters, or favorite people from a certain century.

Halloween masquerade dances with masked are where the people dances with masks on so that the dancers do not know who they are dancing with. It gives the dance an air of mystery because the dancers are hiding their true identities.

Halloween DJs or disc jockeys play music for the dance. Every dance needs great music, so that the dancers can dance to a great beat. The added factor of having a live Disc Jockey makes the party get two thumbs-up by the dancers. The dancers have the chance to a make a request or ask the Disc Jockey the play a particular song and dedicate it to their special friend of spouse. That is so sweet. Sometimes people get engaged during this dedication.

Halloween bands can play for the Halloween dances. This also adds a wow factor to the Halloween Dance. There is something about dancing to live music. These bands are professional musicians and they can play several popular Halloween themed music. The dancers can also like above, make requests. Being able to make requests gives the Halloween Dances the appearance of being personal for the dancers at the Halloween Dance.

Titus Uno, Certified Public Accountant, Forensic Certified Public Accountant, and Chartered Global Management Accountant and the Forensic Certified Public Accountant team: Drew Samson, Dena Hope, Jack "Sheriff" Starr, and Veronica Jackson must investigate the Halloween Planner Company Headquarters' Halloween Dances Division.

Drew Samson used his Private Investigators experience to gain information on the Halloween Planner Company Headquarters' Halloween Dances Division. Drew Samson uses the most high technology available such as: cameras to take pictures, drones to take videos, cell phones to communicate, Global Positioning System chips to track where suspects travel, night vision binoculars that deer hunters use and supersonic listening devices like those used at football games, ear piece combined with shades recorders to communicate with each other, polygraph machines to get to the truth, and wiretaps to gather information about the company, its employees to make it possible to reconstruct the financials and to help assist in the prosecution of the crime. This high technology is exciting to use because spying on people is fun to gain information on the Halloween Planner Company Headquarters' Halloween Dances Division.

Dena Hope uses her programming skills and hacking skills to get information about the Halloween Planner Company so the Dena Hope can investigate the Halloween Planner Company

Headquarters' Halloween Parties Division. Dena Hope has at her disposal a high-technology van that is an undercover vehicle. This way she can move around Los Angeles, California, United States of America.

Dena Hope uses her programming skills and hacking skills to get information about the Halloween Planner Company so the Dena Hope can investigate the Halloween Planner Company Headquarters' Halloween Dances Division.

Jack "Sheriff" Starr, the CEO of the Forensic Certified Public Accountant team, helps the other team members if the other team members need someone else to help them because sometimes it is impossible for one person to complete the task alone. Jack "Sheriff" Starr used his charismatic personality to get other people to talk to him and to get things accomplished. He uses his cowboy charm to investigate the Halloween Planner Company Headquarters' Halloween Parties Division.

Veronica Jackson set up a times for the Forensic Certified Public Accountant team members so that can meet with the employees to investigate the Halloween Planner Company Headquarters' Halloween Parties Division. Veronica Jackson uses her connections to get the Forensic Certified Public Accountant team into see very important people and to get the team special items such as high-technology gadgets that might be needed during the case.

I, Titus Uno, Certified Public Accountant, Forensic Certified Public Accountant, and Chartered Global Management Accountant, will have to investigate the Halloween Planner Company Headquarters' Halloween Dances Division with the help of my Forensic Certified Public Accountant team: Drew Samson, Dena Hope, Jack "Sheriff" Starr, and Veronica Jackson. I, Titus Uno, Certified Public Accountant, Forensic Certified Public Accountant, and Chartered

Global Management Accountant, could not be a lay witness without their help. Thank you, Drew Samson, Dena Hope, Jack "Sheriff" Starr, and Veronica Jackson.

"Orange" Pumpkin called to check on the Halloween Planner Company Headquarters Movies

Accounts, but to her surprise the Movies account had already been completed and the account

had already been sent to another address. This is a nightmare for any company. There is not any

companies that wants to have their profits stolen. This is why I, Titus Uno, Certified Public

Accountant, Forensic Certified Public Accountant, and Chartered Global Management

Accountant, and my team are on the job to investigate the Halloween Planner Company

Headquarters Halloween Movies Division.

The Halloween Planner Company offers a variety of Halloween Movies to clients. It is

amazing how many people show movies in the client's backyard, in the client's house or

mansion, in a rented building, in the park, at the zoo, and in the cemetery.

Movie stars are known for their Halloween Movies parties. It is a great place to meet and

greet with each other, perhaps in costumes, while watching a Halloween movie or two or 3 or

four. The Halloween Planner Company has help plan several of these parties over the years.

Halloween Movies in the client's backyard are convenient for the client because the

Halloween movie is setup right in the client's backyard. The Halloween movie is setup on a

large screen so that everyone there can watch the Halloween movie or movies.

Halloween Movies in the client's house or mansion, like above, are convenient for the client

because the Halloween movie is setup right in the client's backyard. The Halloween movie is

setup on a large screen so that everyone there can watch the Halloween movie or movies. This

option is usually chosen if the clients think that their neighbor will complain about the volume from the movie. However, this can be solved by just inviting the neighborhood if the client does not mind. Otherwise, this option is selected by the client.

Halloween Movies in a rented building is an exciting option because it puts the movie away from the client's house or mansion. The client rents a building that has the capacity to hold the number of invited Halloween guests. The building is decorated Halloween style and the Halloween movie is shown.

Halloween Movies in the park is an exciting place to show a Halloween movie. The park allows the movie watchers to enjoy the outdoor park by walking, jogging, running, playing sports, or whatever they feel like doing. Then the Halloween movie watchers get to watch their Halloween movie.

Halloween Movies at the zoo is a great place to see the animals at the zoo then go to an area near the zoo that has been setup by the Halloween Planner Company. The movie will start at a certain set time so that the people can plan their visit at the zoo and make it to the Halloween movie without rushing.

Halloween Movies in the cemetery is a site that sets the mood for the movie. Cemeteries are willing to allow movie to be shown if the cemetery is in need of some cash monies. Of course, there needs to be a large area that does not have tombstones so that the movie watchers will not be bothered by anything.

Titus Uno, Certified Public Accountant, Forensic Certified Public Accountant, and Chartered Global Management Accountant and the Forensic Certified Public Accountant team: Drew Samson, Dena Hope, Jack "Sheriff" Starr, and Veronica Jackson must investigate the Halloween Planner Company Headquarters' Halloween Movies Division.

Drew Samson used his Private Investigators experience to gain information on the Halloween Planner Company Headquarters' Halloween Movies Division. Drew Samson uses the most high technology available such as: cameras to take pictures, drones to take videos, cell phones to communicate, Global Positioning System chips to track where suspects travel, night vision binoculars that deer hunters use and supersonic listening devices like those used at football games, ear piece combined with shades recorders to communicate with each other, polygraph machines to get to the truth, and wiretaps to gather information about the company, its employees to make it possible to reconstruct the financials and to help assist in the prosecution of the crime. This high technology is exciting to use because spying on people is fun to gain information on the Halloween Planner Company Headquarters' Halloween Movies Division.

Dena Hope uses her programming skills and hacking skills to get information about the Halloween Planner Company so the Dena Hope can investigate the Halloween Planner Company Headquarters' Halloween Movies Division. Dena Hope has at her disposal a high-technology van that is an undercover vehicle. This way she can move around Los Angeles, California, United States of America.

Dena Hope uses her programming skills and hacking skills to get information about the Halloween Planner Company so the Dena Hope can investigate the Halloween Planner Company Headquarters' Halloween Movies Division.

Jack "Sheriff" Starr, the CEO of the Forensic Certified Public Accountant team, helps the other team members if the other team members need someone else to help them because sometimes it is impossible for one person to complete the task alone. Jack "Sheriff" Starr used his charismatic personality to get other people to talk to him and to get things accomplished. He uses his cowboy charm to investigate the Halloween Planner Company Headquarters' Halloween Movies Division.

Veronica Jackson set up a times for the Forensic Certified Public Accountant team members so that can meet with the employees to investigate the Halloween Planner Company Headquarters' Halloween Movies Division. Veronica Jackson uses her connections to get the Forensic Certified Public Accountant team into see very important people and to get the team special items such as high-technology gadgets that might be needed during the case.

I, Titus Uno, Certified Public Accountant, Forensic Certified Public Accountant, and Chartered Global Management Accountant, will have to investigate the Halloween Planner Company Headquarters' Halloween Movies Division with the help of my Forensic Certified Public Accountant team: Drew Samson, Dena Hope, Jack "Sheriff" Starr, and Veronica Jackson. I, Titus Uno, Certified Public Accountant, Forensic Certified Public Accountant, and Chartered Global Management Accountant, could not be a lay witness without their help. Thank you, Drew Samson, Dena Hope, Jack "Sheriff" Starr, and Veronica Jackson.

"Orange" Pumpkin called to check on the Halloween Planner Company Headquarters Cards Accounts, but to her surprise the Cards account had already been completed and the account had already been sent to another address. This is a nightmare for any company. There is not any companies that wants to have their profits stolen. This is why I, Titus Uno, Certified Public Accountant, Forensic Certified Public Accountant, and Chartered Global Management Accountant, and my team are on the job to investigate the Halloween Planner Company Headquarters Halloween Cards Division.

The Halloween Planner Company offers a variety of Halloween Cards to clients. This is a popular Halloween item that is offered by The Halloween Planner Company that people know.

People give Halloween cards to each other. It is a great way to say that the Halloween cards giver is thinking about, or perhaps, even love the recipient of the card.

Ghost cards are part of the Halloween Planner Company Halloween Cards Division. The ghost are flying around and usually say, "Boo." On the cards.

Pumpkin cards are part of the Halloween Planner Company Halloween Cards Division. The pumpkins are always smiling on the cards.

Mummy cards are part of the Halloween Planner Company Halloween Cards Division. The mummies usually say something like, "I want to be your mummy" on the cards.

Bat cards are part of the Halloween Planner Company Halloween Cards Division. The bats usually are flying around on the cards.

Witches cards are part of the Halloween Planner Company Halloween Cards Division. The witches usually have their brooms and brewing pots on the cards.

Spider cards are part of the Halloween Planner Company Halloween Cards Division. The spiders on these cards usually have cute spiders on the cards.

Dracula cards are part of the Halloween Planner Company Halloween Cards Division. Dracula usually says, "I want to drink your blood" on the cards.

Titus Uno, Certified Public Accountant, Forensic Certified Public Accountant, and Chartered Global Management Accountant and the Forensic Certified Public Accountant team: Drew Samson, Dena Hope, Jack "Sheriff" Starr, and Veronica Jackson must investigate the Halloween Planner Company Headquarters' Halloween Cards Division.

Drew Samson used his Private Investigators experience to gain information and on the Halloween Planner Company Headquarters' Halloween Cards Division. Drew Samson uses the most high technology available such as: cameras to take pictures, drones to take videos, cell phones to communicate, Global Positioning System chips to track where suspects travel, night vision binoculars that deer hunters use and supersonic listening devices like those used at football games, ear piece combined with shades recorders to communicate with each other, polygraph machines to get to the truth, and wiretaps to gather information about the company, its employees to make it possible to reconstruct the financials and to help assist in the prosecution of the crime. This high technology is exciting to use because spying on people is fun to gain information on the Halloween Planner Company Headquarters' Halloween Cards Division.

Dena Hope uses her programming skills and hacking skills to get information about the Halloween Planner Company so the Dena Hope can investigate the Halloween Planner Company Headquarters' Halloween Cards Division. Dena Hope has at her disposal a high-technology van that is an undercover vehicle. This way she can move around Los Angeles, California, United States of America.

Dena Hope uses her programming skills and hacking skills to get information about the Halloween Planner Company so the Dena Hope can investigate the Halloween Planner Company Headquarters' Halloween Cards Division.

Jack "Sheriff" Starr, the CEO of the Forensic Certified Public Accountant team, helps the other team members if the other team members need someone else to help them because sometimes it is impossible for one person to complete the task alone. Jack "Sheriff" Starr used his charismatic personality to get other people to talk to him and to get things accomplished. He uses his cowboy charm to investigate the Halloween Planner Company Headquarters' Halloween Cards Division.

Veronica Jackson set up a times for the Forensic Certified Public Accountant team members so that can meet with the employees to investigate the Halloween Planner Company Headquarters' Halloween Cards Division. Veronica Jackson uses her connections to get the Forensic Certified Public Accountant team into see very important people and to get the team special items such as high-technology gadgets that might be needed during the case.

Jack "Sheriff" Starr, the CEO of the Forensic Certified Public Accountant team, helps the other team members if the other team members need someone else to help them because sometimes it is impossible for one person to complete the task alone. Jack "Sheriff" Starr used his charismatic personality to get other people to talk to him and to get things accomplished. He uses his cowboy charm to investigate the Halloween Planner Company Headquarters' Halloween Cards Division.

Veronica Jackson set up a times for the Forensic Certified Public Accountant team members so that can meet with the employees to investigate the Halloween Planner Company Headquarters' Halloween Cards Division. Veronica Jackson uses her connections to get the Forensic Certified Public Accountant team into see very important people and to get the team special items such as high-technology gadgets that might be needed during the case.

I, Titus Uno, Certified Public Accountant, Forensic Certified Public Accountant, and Chartered Global Management Accountant, will have to investigate the Halloween Planner Company Headquarters' Halloween Cards Division with the help of my Forensic Certified Public Accountant team: Drew Samson, Dena Hope, Jack "Sheriff" Starr, and Veronica Jackson. I, Titus Uno, Certified Public Accountant, Forensic Certified Public Accountant, and Chartered Global Management Accountant, could not be a lay witness without their help. Thank you, Drew Samson, Dena Hope, Jack "Sheriff" Starr, and Veronica Jackson.

"Orange" Pumpkin called to check on the Halloween Planner Company Headquarters Mazes Accounts, but to her surprise the Mazes account had already been completed and the account had already been sent to another address. This is a nightmare for any company. There is not any companies that wants to have their profits stolen. This is why I, Titus Uno, Certified Public Accountant, Forensic Certified Public Accountant, and Chartered Global Management Accountant, and my team are on the job to investigate the Halloween Planner Company Headquarters Halloween Mazes Division.

The Halloween Planner Company has several farms that use their cornfields to form Mazes patterns so that people can come to their corn fields and go through the Mazes. The farmers use boards to form the predetermined maze patterns, that way the corn does not grow where the boards are placed. This means that where the boards are placed, the corn will not have to be planted, watered, and then plowed down to make the path for the brave people that dare to enter the amazing corn mazes.

The people that show up enjoy riding on hayrides to the entrance of the cornfield mazes. It is so fun to sit on hay and have the breeze of the wind hit your face. If it is nighttime you can look up and see the stars filling the sky. It is so hard to see the stars in the big city. I think that is why so many people that rides the hayride and enter the cornfield maze. As the customers go through the maze these stars make a pretty awesome natural ceiling helping to light their way through this cornfield maze. It is exciting not knowing what waits around every corner.

Groups of people arrive by chartered buses, school buses, tour buses, church buses, cars, vans, and a few by limousines. It is so fun to arrive at the cornfield maze as a group. It is so exiting to have several people to go through the maze with each other. After they leave the maze that are all so excited.

Families with children have a blast going through the cornfield maze. Of course, the children have to pick on each other. The parents have fun being with each other, however, the parents have to keep an eye on their children to make sure that they are having fun going through the cornfield maze.

Families that are having family reunions go through the cornfield maze with their family that all have the same last name. Large families are exciting to have at the cornfield maze. The family reunion events are setup close to the entrance. That way they can go in and out to eat food, get something to drink or to do a family reunion activity. This is where each separate part of the whole family compete against each other.

Couples date and hold hands as they enter the cornfield maze, they hold hands while they go through the cornfield maze, they are still holding hands when they come out of the cornfield maze, and they hold hands as they leave the cornfield maze entrance or exit area.

The Halloween Planner Company Headquarters places several Halloween decorations in the mazes. No one knows what awaits them as they go around to corner. Maybe, a dead end, oh no, you have to turnaround. Maybe, there are spider webs. Maybe, there are zombies. Maybe, there are ghosts. There might be black cats. There might be cracked mirrors.

Titus Uno, Certified Public Accountant, Forensic Certified Public Accountant, and Chartered Global Management Accountant and the Forensic Certified Public Accountant team: Drew

Samson, Dena Hope, Jack "Sheriff" Starr, and Veronica Jackson must investigate the Halloween Planner Company Headquarters' Halloween Mazes Division.

Drew Samson used his Private Investigators experience to gain information on the Halloween Planner Company Headquarters' Halloween Mazes Division. Drew Samson uses the most high technology available such as: cameras to take pictures, drones to take videos, cell phones to communicate, Global Positioning System chips to track where suspects travel, night vision binoculars that deer hunters use and supersonic listening devices like those used at football games, ear piece combined with shades recorders to communicate with each other, polygraph machines to get to the truth, and wiretaps to gather information about the company, its employees to make it possible to reconstruct the financials and to help assist in the prosecution of the crime. This high technology is exciting to use because spying on people is fun to gain information on the Halloween Planner Company Headquarters' Halloween Mazes Division.

Dena Hope uses her programming skills and hacking skills to get information about the Halloween Planner Company so the Dena Hope can investigate the Halloween Planner Company Headquarters' Halloween Mazes Division. Dena Hope has at her disposal a high-technology van that is an undercover vehicle. This way she can move around Los Angeles, California, United States of America.

Dena Hope uses her programming skills and hacking skills to get information about the Halloween Planner Company so the Dena Hope can investigate the Halloween Planner Company Headquarters' Halloween Mazes Division.

Jack "Sheriff" Starr, the CEO of the Forensic Certified Public Accountant team, helps the other team members if the other team members need someone else to help them because sometimes it is impossible for one person to complete the task alone. Jack "Sheriff" Starr used his charismatic personality to get other people to talk to him and to get things accomplished. He uses his cowboy charm to investigate the Halloween Planner Company Headquarters' Halloween Mazes Division.

Veronica Jackson set up a times for the Forensic Certified Public Accountant team members so that can meet with the employees to investigate the Halloween Planner Company Headquarters' Halloween Mazes Division. Veronica Jackson uses her connections to get the Forensic Certified Public Accountant team into see very important people and to get the team special items such as high-technology gadgets that might be needed during the case.

Jack "Sheriff" Starr, the CEO of the Forensic Certified Public Accountant team, helps the other team members if the other team members need someone else to help them because sometimes it is impossible for one person to complete the task alone. Jack "Sheriff" Starr used his charismatic personality to get other people to talk to him and to get things accomplished. He uses his cowboy charm to investigate the Halloween Planner Company Headquarters' Halloween Mazes Division.

Veronica Jackson set up a times for the Forensic Certified Public Accountant team members so that can meet with the employees to investigate the Halloween Planner Company Headquarters' Halloween Mazes Division. Veronica Jackson uses her connections to get the Forensic Certified Public Accountant team into see very important people and to get the team special items such as high-technology gadgets that might be needed during the case.

I, Titus Uno, Certified Public Accountant, Forensic Certified Public Accountant, and Chartered Global Management Accountant, will have to investigate the Halloween Planner Company Headquarters' Halloween Mazes Division with the help of my Forensic Certified Public Accountant team: Drew Samson, Dena Hope, Jack "Sheriff" Starr, and Veronica Jackson.

I, Titus Uno, Certified Public Accountant, Forensic Certified Public Accountant, and Chartered Global Management Accountant, could not be a lay witness without their help. Thank you, Drew Samson, Dena Hope, Jack "Sheriff" Starr, and Veronica Jackson.

Chapter 15 the Jack-O-Lanterns and Pumpkin Patches Accounting for These Accounts

"Orange" Pumpkin called to check on the Halloween Planner Company Headquarters Pumpkins and Jack-O-Lanterns Accounts, but to her surprise the Pumpkins and Jack-O-Lanterns account had already been completed and the account had already been sent to another address. This is a nightmare for any company. There is not any companies that wants to have their profits stolen. This is why I, Titus Uno, Certified Public Accountant, Forensic Certified Public Accountant, and Chartered Global Management Accountant, and my team are on the job to investigate the Halloween Planner Company Headquarters Halloween Pumpkins and Jack-O-Lanterns Division.

The Halloween Planner Company offers a variety of Jack-O-Lanterns and pumpkin patches packages to clients. Pumpkins and Jack-O-Lanterns are an important object or symbol of Halloween.

There are pumpkin carving tables set up for people to carve pumping that the customers themselves have pulled a pumpkin or some people pick ones that other customers or Halloween Planner Company have pulled.

There are pumpkin pie eating contests that are set up at the pumpkin patches. It is amazing that there is never a problem of finding people to enter the contest. People love to eat pumpkin pies. The contest is to see who can eat the most pies in 5 minutes. It is funny to watch all the pie eaters eat the pie with their hands behind their back. Some people really get into the pumpkin pies and their faces are a mess when the contest is stopped after 5minutes. The winners get an orange ribbon and has bragging rights all day.

Pumpkin patches are very popular during Halloween. People like to ride on a hayride to get to the pumpkin patches. Some of the people pick pumpkins to pull for the purpose of taking it home and others to carve it into a Jack-O-Lanterns.

Titus Uno, Certified Public Accountant, Forensic Certified Public Accountant, and Chartered Global Management Accountant and the Forensic Certified Public Accountant team: Drew Samson, Dena Hope, Jack "Sheriff" Starr, and Veronica Jackson must investigate the Halloween Planner Company Headquarters Halloween Jack-O-Lanterns and Pumpkin Patches Division.

Drew Samson used his Private Investigators experience to gain information on the Halloween Planner Company Headquarters' Halloween Jack-O-Lanterns and Pumpkin Patches Division. Drew Samson uses the most high technology available such as: cameras to take pictures, drones to take videos, cell phones to communicate, Global Positioning System chips to track where suspects travel, night vision binoculars that deer hunters use and supersonic listening devices like those used at football games, ear piece combined with shades recorders to communicate with each other, polygraph machines to get to the truth, and wiretaps to gather information about the company, its employees to make it possible to reconstruct the financials and to help assist in the prosecution of the crime. This high technology is exciting to use because spying on people is fun to gain information on the Halloween Planner Company Headquarters' Halloween Jack-O-Lanterns and Pumpkin Patches Divisions.

Dena Hope uses her programming skills and hacking skills to get information about the Halloween Planner Company so the Dena Hope can investigate the Halloween Planner Company Headquarters' Halloween Jack-O-Lanterns and Pumpkin Patches Division. Dena Hope has at her disposal a high-technology van that is an undercover vehicle. This way she can move around Los Angeles, California, United States of America.

Drew Samson uses the most high technology available such as: cameras to take pictures, drones to take videos, cell phones to communicate, Global Positioning System chips to track where suspects travel, night vision binoculars that deer hunters use and supersonic listening devices like those used at football games, ear piece combined with shades recorders to communicate with each other, polygraph machines to get to the truth, and wiretaps to gather information about the company, its employees to make it possible to reconstruct the financials and to help assist in the prosecution of the crime. This high technology is exciting to use because spying on people is fun to gain information on the Halloween Planner Company Headquarters' Halloween Pumpkins and Jack-O-Lanterns Division.

Dena Hope uses her programming skills and hacking skills to get information about the Halloween Planner Company so the Dena Hope can investigate the Halloween Planner Company Headquarters' Halloween Pumpkins and Jack-O-Lanterns Division. Dena Hope has at her disposal a high-technology van that is an undercover vehicle. This way she can move around Los Angeles, California, United States of America.

Dena Hope uses her programming skills and hacking skills to get information about the Halloween Planner Company so the Dena Hope can investigate the Halloween Planner Company Headquarters' Halloween Jack-O-Lanterns and Pumpkin Patches Division.

Jack "Sheriff" Starr, the CEO of the Forensic Certified Public Accountant team, helps the other team members if the other team members need someone else to help them because sometimes it is impossible for one person to complete the task alone. Jack "Sheriff" Starr used his charismatic personality to get other people to talk to him and to get things accomplished. He uses his cowboy charm to investigate the Halloween Planner Company Headquarters' Halloween Pumpkins and Jack-O-Lanterns Division.

Veronica Jackson set up a times for the Forensic Certified Public Accountant team members so that can meet with the employees to investigate the Halloween Planner Company Headquarters' Halloween Pumpkins and Jack-O-Lanterns Division. Veronica Jackson uses her connections to get the Forensic Certified Public Accountant team into see very important people and to get the team special items such as high-technology gadgets that might be needed during the case.

I, Titus Uno, Certified Public Accountant, Forensic Certified Public Accountant, and Chartered Global Management Accountant, will have to investigate the Halloween Planner Company Headquarters' Halloween Jack-O-Lanterns and Pumpkin Patches Division with the help of my Forensic Certified Public Accountant team: Drew Samson, Dena Hope, Jack "Sheriff" Starr, and Veronica Jackson. I, Titus Uno, Certified Public Accountant, Forensic Certified Public Accountant, and Chartered Global Management Accountant, could not be a lay witness without their help. Thank you, Drew Samson, Dena Hope, Jack "Sheriff" Starr, and Veronica Jackson.

Officer Chuck Mac, from The Royal Canadian Mounted Police, Agent "Davy" Bond, from the Federal Bureau of Investigation, Agent "Super" Vision, from the Central Intelligence Agency, and Agent "Spider" Webb, from the Homeland Security are all on the scene here in Los Angeles, California, United States of America.

As described in *The Forensic Certified Public Accountant and the Cremated 64-SQUARES Financial Statements* - book number one: These government agencies work with the police and each other, however, the agencies via for jurisdiction, to see who has the authority to perform the investigation. The Royal Canadian Mounted Police works with the Federal Bureau of Investigation, the Central Intelligence Agency, and the Homeland Security all work well together to protect the public of both Canada and the United States of America from being threatened by terrorists with the goal of blowing-up buildings with people inside. There might be some be disagreement on who is top dog, but it is decided by the people high up on the totem pole. Once, that is figured out, all the agents and mounted police join forces to bring the terrorist to justice before the terrorist targets are hit with explosives.

As described in *The Forensic Certified Public Accountant and the Cremated 64-SQUARES Financial Statements* - book number one: Officer Chuck Mac, from The Royal Canadian Mounted Police, has a keen sense of direction. The Royal Canadian Mounted Police are famous for wearing their red uniforms with their black boots and their hats with the big rims. They usually ride horses on the trails, but they do also ride in vehicles on the roads.

As described in *The Forensic Certified Public Accountant and the Cremated 64-SQUARES Financial Statements* - book number one: Agent "Davy" Bond, from the Federal Bureau of

Investigation, is a great agent that entered the FBI right after he obtained his college degree. Agent "Davy" Bond likes to wear dark shades with his perfectly pressed black business suit and black spotless polished shiny shoes. Agent "Davy" Bond always has an earpiece in his right ear and his gun in his shoulder holster under the left side of his suit coat. Agent "Davy" Bond is an excellent sharp shooter with a rifle and even better with his gun. Agent "Davy" Bond may miss one out of 200 shots, sometimes one out of 300. That is where Agent "Davy" Bond got the nick name of 'Davy.' Agent "Davy" Bond also enjoys memorizing mug shot of wanted criminals. Agent "Davy" Bond always says, 'You never know when you might come face-to-face with a wanted criminal, and it would be terrible to just let them walk away because you did not recognize their face.' When I, Titus Uno, Certified Public Accountant, Forensic Certified Public Accountant, and Chartered Global Management Accountant, heard his say this, I thought to myself 'That is a very long quote, but it is true.'

As described in *The Forensic Certified Public Accountant and the Cremated 64-SQUARES Financial Statements* - book number one: Agent "Super" Vision, from the Central Intelligence Agency, has an awesome background in criminology. Agent "Super" Vision is what you would call a profiler. Agent "Super" Vision got her nickname "Super" because Agent "Super" Vision is super at her job. Plus it is pretty funny. That is Central Intelligence agencies humor. I, Titus Uno, Certified Public Accountant, Forensic Certified Public Accountant, and Chartered Global Management Accountant, think that it is really funny. So I, Titus Uno, Certified Public Accountant, Forensic Certified Public Accountant, and Chartered Global Management Accountant, guess it is also Forensic Certified Public Accountant humor. People can ask, "Do you need "Super" Vision to help you with what you are doing?" Agent "Super" Vision has a knack for understanding how and what a particular criminal is thinking just by looking at their psych file. I, Titus Uno, Certified Public Accountant, Forensic Certified Public Accountant, and Chartered Global Management Accountant, was very impressed the first time that I saw Agent "Super" Vision in action doing this very thing. Agent "Super" Vision looked at a file for about a minute and then told other agents where the criminal could be located. I, Titus Uno, Certified Public Accountant, Forensic Certified Public Accountant, and Chartered Global Management Accountant, am good at doing this, but I, Titus Uno, Certified Public Accountant, Forensic Certified Public Accountant, and Chartered Global Management Accountant, takes me a little more time to digest the information. I think that I can hold my own just fine and find a criminal in my own style.

As described in *The Forensic Certified Public Accountant and the Cremated 64-SQUARES Financial Statements* - book number one: Agent "Spider" Webb, from Homeland Security, is a hard person to figure out in a hurry. He is what you would say very quiet and has a great poker face. If I, Titus Uno, Certified Public Accountant, Forensic Certified Public Accountant, and Chartered Global Management Accountant, were you, I would not play poker with him in the game, unless you are dying to be separated from you wad of cash. I, Titus Uno, Certified Public Accountant, Forensic Certified Public Accountant, and Chartered Global Management Accountant, have be around him for several days and he has yet to crack a smile. Like the other agent and mounted police, he has an excellent background in understanding a criminal and the ability to track them down and make an arrest. He got his nickname, "Spider" because he is the best at setting up traps to catch criminals. They fall into his traps without even knowing that they have. Then before they know it they are under arrest and thrown in jail. Then it is up to the court system to keep the criminal in the prison for a very long time. However, our job is to catch the criminals and help the court system decide that our evidence is enough to arrive at a guilty verdict.

As described in *The Forensic Certified Public Accountant and the Cremated 64-SQUARES Financial Statements* - book number one: Titus Uno Certified Public Accountant, Forensic Certified Public Accountant, and Chartered Global Management Accountant and the Forensic Certified Public Accountant team: Drew Samson, Dena Hope, and Veronica Jackson must interact with Officer Chuck Mac, from The Royal Canadian Mounted Police, Agent "Davy" Bond, from the Federal Bureau of Investigation, Agent "Super" Vision, from the Central Intelligence Agency, and Agent "Spider" Webb, from Homeland Security.

As described in *The Forensic Certified Public Accountant and the Cremated 64-SQUARES Financial Statements* - book number one: Drew Samson used his Private Investigators experience to communicate with Officer Chuck Mac, from The Royal Canadian Mounted Police, Agent "Davy" Bond, from the Federal Bureau of Investigation, Agent "Super" Vision, from the Central Intelligence Agency, and Agent "Spider" Webb, from Homeland Security. This takes great skill because, Drew Samson is dealing with a National Officer and three National Agents. They are not always able to share information with us even though we have 64-SQUARES's permission to question or interrogate people that we need to. Drew Samson does stay up to date because Drew Samson has a friendly voice, and people like to talk to him.

As described in *The Forensic Certified Public Accountant and the Cremated 64-SQUARES Financial Statements* - book number one: Dena Hope used her programming skills and hacking skills carefully to gain information from The Royal Canadian Mounted Police, from the Federal Bureau of Investigation, from the Central Intelligence Agency, and from the Homeland Security.

As described in *The Forensic Certified Public Accountant and the Cremated 64-SQUARES Financial Statements* - book number one: Veronica Jackson sets up appointment times for us to visit with Officer Chuck Mac, from The Royal Canadian Mounted Police, Agent "Davy" Bond, from the Federal Bureau of Investigation, Agent "Super" Vision, from the Central Intelligence Agency, and Agent "Spider" Webb, from Homeland Security.

As described in *The Forensic Certified Public Accountant and the Cremated 64-SQUARES Financial Statements* - book number one: I, Titus Uno, Certified Public Accountant, Forensic Certified Public Accountant, and Chartered Global Management Accountant, have to stay up to date and Officer Chuck Mac, from The Royal Canadian Mounted Police, Agent "Davy" Bond, from the Federal Bureau of Investigation, Agent "Super" Vision, from the Central Intelligence Agency, and Agent "Spider" Webb, from Homeland Security are a great source of important information. They have so many people that are working on gathering information.

The reason that Officer Chuck Mac, from The Royal Canadian Mounted Police, Agent "Davy" Bond, from the Federal Bureau of Investigation, Agent "Super" Vision, from the Central Intelligence Agency, and Agent "Spider" Webb, from the Homeland Security are all on the scene here in Los Angeles, California, United States of America is because Clef Treble has escaped from prison and is in Los Angeles, California, United States of America. Clef Treble has the ability to escape from any location without very much effort. The plot thickens, but this was the key that allowed the pieces to fit together.

Judge Henry Law enters the courtroom to hear the case of the Halloween "identity theft ghost employee" because Clef Treble is being accused of identity theft and being a ghost employee. Judge Henry Law is a very strict Judge when it comes to criminals.

The prosecutor in this case is Mr. Square Circle. He got this name because he can make a square object fit into a circle. Once a criminal is caught the criminal might as well get used to spending time behind bars. Mr. Square Circle works his magic at every criminal that he has prosecuted has gone to jail.

This case is well-prepared by Mr. Square Circle. He has the evidence and testimony from Officer Chuck Mac, from The Royal Canadian Mounted Police, Agent "Davy" Bond, from the Federal Bureau of Investigation, Agent "Super" Vision, from the Central Intelligence Agency, and Agent "Spider" Webb, from the Homeland Security. Their testimony along with my Forensic Certified Public Accountant testimony makes the Prosecutor Square Circle's case very well-prepared for a guilty verdict.

I, Titus Uno, Certified Public Accountant, Forensic Certified Public Accountant, Chartered Global Management Accountant, entered the courtroom and took the stand. I raised my left hand in the oath position and placed my fight hand on the Holy Bible. I said to the judge, bailiff, and to the courtroom, "I solemnly promise and swear to tell the truth, the whole truth, and only the truth, so help me God." I sat down in the lay witness chair and I was ready to testify about the facts of the financial statements.

Mr Square Circle told me, "Mr Uno, please testify as to the amount that the Halloween Planner Company Headquarters lost because of Clef Treble." I testified, "That the Halloween Planner Company Headquarters lost $3,923,728.16 because of the theft of revenue that Clef Treble stole from the Halloween Planner Company. This is the entire amount of revenue that the Halloween Planner Company earns. The Halloween Planner Company only collects the money in October, this is the month that Halloween occurs."

Since the defendant was convinced that he was going to get a guilty verdict and be sent to a maximum security prison so that he could not escape again. The defendant, Clef Treble made a deal to return to the prison with the stipulation that Clef Treble return all the monies to the Halloween Planner Company. This would return the Halloween Planner Company Headquarters cash and accounts receivable accounts to the corrected amount. That being the amount before Clef Treble took the monies from the Halloween Planner Company by having their clients send the monies to an address the Clef Treble had set up to collect the monies.

Clef Treble said that he only took the money to lure me, Titus Uno, Certified Public Accountant, Forensic Certified Public Accountant, Chartered Global Management Accountant, and my team to Los Angeles, California, United States of America.

Sometime court cases are setter outside of the courtroom. This case was settled the best way that it could have been settled. The Halloween Planner Company gets their money, and Clef Treble, the "identity theft ghost employee," gets to avoid the maximum security prison.

Judge Henry Law told Clef Treble that if he decides to break out of his prison again, when caught he well go straight to the maximum security prison. That this is Clef Treble's last chance to avoid the maximum security prison. Judge Henry Law then hit the gavel and said, "Case

closed!"

What a case, I, Titus Uno, Certified Public Accountant, Forensic Certified Public Accountant, and Chartered Global Management Accountant, never dreamed that the "identity theft ghost employee" was actually going to turn out to be Clef Treble. Once, Officer Chuck Mac, from The Royal Canadian Mounted Police, Agent "Davy" Bond, from the Federal Bureau of Investigation, Agent "Super" Vision, from the Central Intelligence Agency, and Agent "Spider" Webb, from the Homeland Security are all on the scene here in Los Angeles, California, United States of America is because Clef Treble has escaped from prison and is in Los Angeles, California, United States of America. It was great to be able to see Officer Chuck Mac, from The Royal Canadian Mounted Police, Agent "Davy" Bond, from the Federal Bureau of Investigation, Agent "Super" Vision, from the Central Intelligence Agency, and Agent "Spider" Webb, from the Homeland Security again.

That is when the pieces fell into place when Officer Chuck Mac, from The Royal Canadian Mounted Police, Agent "Davy" Bond, from the Federal Bureau of Investigation, Agent "Super" Vision, from the Central Intelligence Agency, and Agent "Spider" Webb, from the Homeland Security told me that Clef Treble had escaped. Clef Treble was not in my equation in the calculation of the guilty person who was the "identity theft ghost employee" because everyone thought that he was still behind bars.

Clef wanted to lure me and my team to come to Los Angeles, California, United States of America. It did not take long to figure out that Clef Treble was also "Patch" MacGoo. Clef is a master of disguise and a great cat burglar. Clef Treble was under the impression that if we were out of our element that he could out fox me, Titus Uno, Certified Public Accountant, Forensic Certified Public Accountant, and Chartered Global Management Accountant and my Forensic Certified Public Accountant team.

Autumn Fall, the CEO or the Chief Executive Officer of the Halloween Planner Company has decided that she will stay at the Halloween Planner Company Headquarters for several years. Her family enjoys living in Los Angeles, California, United States of America and are very happy. She also enjoys working with Spring Summer, the CFO or the Chief Financial Officer of the Halloween Planner Company, and "Orange" Pumpkin, Account Manager of the Halloween Planner Company.

Spring Summer, the CFO or the Chief Financial Officer of the Halloween Planner Company has also decided that she will stay at the Halloween Planner Company Headquarters. Los Angeles, California, United States of America. Spring Summer has a blast working with Autumn Fall, the CEO or the Chief Executive Officer of the Halloween Planner Company and "Orange" Pumpkin, Accounts Manager of the Halloween Planner Company.

Autumn Fall, the CEO or the Chief Executive Officer of the Halloween Planner Company, and Spring Summer, the CFO or the Chief Financial Officer of the Halloween Planner Company, plan to stay co-worker friends forever or as long as they can. Their families are very close and the families are always getting together to do activities all year round. It is the perfect friendship that anyone could ask to get.

"Orange" Pumpkin, Accounts Manager of the Halloween Planner Company has decided that she will also stay at the Halloween Planner Company Headquarters. "Orange" Pumpkin, enjoys working as Accounts Manager collecting and talking to the clients. "Orange" Pumpkin gets to meet every client that the Halloween Planner Company has as a client.

Titus Uno, Certified Public Accountant, Forensic Certified Public Accountant, and Chartered Global Management Accountant and the Forensic Certified Public Accountant team: Drew Samson, Dena Hope, Jack "Sheriff" Starr, and Veronica Jackson investigated the Halloween Planner Company to find out who the identity theft ghost employee really was and to help restore the Halloween Planner Company Headquarters revenue be back to the actual amount that it should be in the Halloween Planner Company Headquarters income statement. Without the revenue being in the income statement, there would only be expenses. That is not great for any company.

Drew Samson used his Private Investigators experience to gain information on the Halloween Planner Company. Drew Samson uses the most high technology available such as: cameras to take pictures, drones to take videos, cell phones to communicate, Global Positioning System chips to track where suspects travel, night vision binoculars that deer hunters use and supersonic listening devices like those used at football games, ear piece combined with shades recorders to communicate with each other, polygraph machines to get to the truth, and wiretaps to gather information about the company, its employees to make it possible to reconstruct the financials and to help assist in the prosecution of the crime. This high technology is exciting to use because spying on people is fun to gain information on the Halloween Planner Company.

Dena Hope uses her programming skills and hacking skills to get information about the Halloween Planner Company. Dena Hope has at her disposal a high-technology van that is an undercover vehicle. This way she can move around Los Angeles, California, United States of

America to find out who the identity theft ghost employee really was and to help restore the

Halloween Planner Company Headquarters revenue

Drew Samson uses the most high technology available such as: cameras to take pictures, drones to take videos, cell phones to communicate, Global Positioning System chips to track where suspects travel, night vision binoculars that deer hunters use and supersonic listening devices like those used at football games, ear piece combined with shades recorders to communicate with each other, polygraph machines to get to the truth, and wiretaps to gather information about the company, its employees to make it possible to reconstruct the financials and to help assist in the prosecution of the crime. This high technology is exciting to use because spying on people is fun to gain information on the Halloween Planner Company Headquarters' Halloween Pumpkins and Jack-O-Lanterns Division.

Jack "Sheriff" Starr, the CEO of the Forensic Certified Public Accountant team, helps the other team members if the other team members need someone else to help them because sometimes it is impossible for one person to complete the task alone. Jack "Sheriff" Starr used his charismatic personality to get other people to talk to him and to get things accomplished. He uses his cowboy charm to investigate the Halloween Planner Company to find out who the identity theft ghost employee really was and to help restore the Halloween Planner Company Headquarters revenue.

Veronica Jackson set up a times for the Forensic Certified Public Accountant team members so that can meet with the employees to investigate the Halloween Planner Company. Veronica Jackson uses her connections to get the Forensic Certified Public Accountant team into see very important people and to get the team special items such as high-technology gadgets that might be needed during the case to find out who the identity theft ghost employee really was and to help restore the Halloween Planner Company Headquarters revenue and thus allow the Halloween Planner Company to continue to help everyone enjoy Halloween.

I, Titus Uno, Certified Public Accountant, Forensic Certified Public Accountant, and Chartered Global Management Accountant, will have to investigate the Halloween Planner Company with the help of my Forensic Certified Public Accountant team: Drew Samson, Dena Hope, Jack "Sheriff" Starr, and Veronica Jackson. I, Titus Uno, Certified Public Accountant, Forensic Certified Public Accountant, and Chartered Global Management Accountant, could not be a lay witness without their help. Thank you, Drew Samson, Dena Hope, Jack "Sheriff" Starr, and Veronica Jackson. Another case has been closed and the "identity theft ghost employee" or Clef Treble is back behind bars, or is he?

www.ingramcontent.com/pod-product-compliance
Lightning Source LLC
Chambersburg PA
CBHW080643180526
45168CB00008B/3288

* 9 7 8 1 5 1 9 0 1 6 5 6 0 *